About the Authors

Marshall's Story: When I started college, my goal was to save as much time and money as possible. I had a crazy idea to make that happen. I would try to graduate in half the time, two years instead of four, and at half the cost. My peers and teachers thought it was impossible. Some even laughed. After all, they had a point: I wasn't special. I was just an eighteen-year-old kid with learning disabilities, autism, and an average IQ. Throughout school, I struggled with math, writing, and foreign languages. I worked hard to compensate for my shortcomings and graduated with honors from Stevenson in Pebble Beach, California. In the fall of 2020, I started college with no transfer credits. While taking twenty-seven college credits most semesters, I worked part-time in my family's business, trained twenty-plus hours weekly for triathlons, and finished two 140.6-mile Ironman races. Two years later, in spring 2022, I set a record for the fastest graduation in the University of Tampa's (UT) history. At UT, I earned a 3.98 overall GPA and a Bachelor of Science in Entrepreneurship. Today, I manage my family's industrial real estate properties, compete in ultra-endurance races, and build businesses with Marcus. Marcus and I met in high school and instantly bonded over our shared passion for business and teaching people about financial literacy. As friends and business partners, we do three things.

1. **Teach young people the essential life skills they need to succeed.**
2. **Help successful individuals grow their wealth for generations to come.**
3. **Work with business owners to help them reach their biggest goals.**

Marcus's Story: I grew up in Pebble Beach, California, and faced significant challenges early in life. One of my earliest memories was losing my mother to cervical cancer when I was just four years old. My father, a dedicated dermatologist, raised me while balancing his demanding career. He was my hero, deeply committed to his patients and passionate about his work. I spent countless hours in his clinic, working to follow in his footsteps. In my family, as in many Asian families, achievement wasn't just encouraged. It was expected. Everything changed when my father was diagnosed with stage-four prostate cancer. After a five-year battle, he passed away. I was left to navigate my teenage years without my parents. This dark and challenging time forced me to mature quickly. Without pressure from family expectations, I had to define what success meant to me. I began to explore my true passions: entrepreneurship and wrestling. Both pursuits required resilience, strategy, and mental toughness. I embraced these qualities and used them to rebuild my life. At Carmel High School in California, I maximized every opportunity. I led clubs, took dual enrollment classes, AP exams, and summer college courses. I also helped students get scholarships. After high school, I attended the University of Southern California (USC) on a full scholarship. Using the college credits I earned in high school, I finished a Bachelor of Science in Accounting and a Master of Science in Finance in four years instead of the typical six.

Our Dream: Accelerating Lifelong Student Success

Our dream is to give students the resources they need to excel in school and achieve lifelong success after graduation doing the work they love. To accomplish this mission, we focus on teaching essential strategies, habits, and life skills—such as financial literacy—that are critically important yet often missing from traditional education. We'll do our part to fill the gaps in education and empower students to achieve tremendous success in all areas of their lives. To make this dream a reality, we need your support. You can help by sharing this book, leaving a review, visiting AtlasClass.com, and connecting with us on YouTube, Instagram, Facebook, and other social media platforms @AtlasClass. Thank you so much for helping spread the word!

ATLAS CLASS

Our Solution for Schools, Teachers, Students, and Parents

To help as many people as possible, we offer many of our educational materials for free so that every student, parent, teacher, and school can afford them. We also provide helpful resources like this book, teachers' materials, and more at affordable prices. Many schools are now required to teach financial literacy; our programs can help meet those requirements. If your local school or organization could benefit from our cost-effective life skills and financial literacy programs, please contact us via email. Together, we can make a real difference in preparing students for a successful future.

To better support you, please let us know:

1. The organization's name, address, and your affiliation.
2. Who we should contact and the best way to reach them
3. How you think we can best serve them?

Email To Contact: Info@AtlasClass.com

Premium Support for Navigating College and Life

We offer premium coaching services to help students, parents, and families navigate the many complexities and challenges of the college process. Our specialized services will help guide you every step of the way from high school to college graduation and beyond with less stress and greater success. We also provide life coaching for individuals trying to find their direction or reach their next big goal. Lastly, we offer speaking engagements and consulting services tailored to your organization's needs. Set up your free informational session today by emailing and letting us know how we can best help you achieve your goals.

Contents

Dedication

To every student who has big dreams and will stop at nothing to make them a reality.
And to everyone who supports students in ways big and small.

The Mission

This book's goal is simple: to show you a better, faster, and more affordable way to earn a college degree and build positive habits for lifelong success.

Now, let's be honest with ourselves. The system we've been told to follow, the one that says, "Go to college, rack up debt, and hope you find a job afterwards," is broken. But there's another way. A smarter way that won't leave you drowning in debt or wasting the best years of your life. The tested and proven strategies in this book are the answers you've been looking for. We saved hundreds of thousands of dollars using the strategies in this book. They reduced our college costs and helped us accelerate our careers. The same strategies that worked for us will work for you. The only thing between you and those results is action, so dig into this book, learn everything you can, and act!

The 5 Core Ideas of This Book

1. **Holistic Success:** Success is about more than good grades or a diploma. It's about victory in all areas of life: mental, emotional, physical, and financial. This book isn't just about school. It's about creating an extraordinary life for yourself.

2. **Guidance and Knowledge:** The path to college is confusing, and the many choices you have to make can be stressful. This book is packed with easy-to-follow tips and advice that will help you navigate the journey with less stress and more confidence.

3. **Affordability:** Let's talk about money. College is expensive! But what if college could be far more affordable? This book shows you how to reduce the time and cost of college. It will help you maximize every minute and stretch every dollar.

4. **Comprehensiveness:** College success doesn't start the day you step onto a college campus. It begins long before that. That's why this book covers the whole process, from middle school to college graduation—and beyond. You'll have all the necessary tools and strategies no matter where you start. This book also has structured questions at the end of each chapter for you to consider, answer, and use to create your action plan.

5. **Personalization:** There's no one-size-fits-all when it comes to education. Every student is different. This book recognizes students' uniqueness and has strategies that will work for you. It doesn't matter if you are academically gifted or struggle with school. It also doesn't matter if you have a lot of resources or few. This book will meet you where you are and help take you where you want to go.

Using This Book to Meet Your Needs

We recommend you download the audio version of this book from our website so you can listen and read simultaneously. Reading plus listening will help you stay focused, read faster, and retain more information. We do this for all the books we read, and we encourage you to try it. While reading and listening, remember that your situation is unique. No one knows your goals and the challenges you face better than you. This book has many strategies. Some will apply to you. Others will not. So, focus on the sections that will help you most.

Already in college? Skip the chapters aimed at younger students.

Are you worried it's too late to start? Don't be. Marshall didn't use these strategies until after he started college. He still graduated in two years.

1. **Everyone Is Different.** Choose your own goals. Challenge yourself but be thoughtful. Push yourself too hard, and you'll experience burnout. Set ambitious goals and modify them as needed.

2. **Every School Is Different.** Know your options. The school you choose can make your journey easier or harder. The key is to pick a school that helps you graduate early rather than slowing you down. Some colleges are flexible, accepting transfer credits and allowing students to take heavier course loads. Others? Not so much. The more flexible the school, the more strategies you can use to graduate faster and save money. However, you may still have options even if you're at a less flexible school. This book will provide valuable strategies and guidance no matter what school you attend.

   Look for Schools That

   - Accept transfer, AP, and dual enrollment credits.
   - Allow you to take more courses per semester.
   - Have classes you can take over winter, spring, and summer breaks.

3. **Data Changes, but Principles Stay the Same:** Let's discuss numbers. The data and figures in this book are based on information at the time of writing. However, we all know that college costs are likely to continue rising. That's the nature of inflation. But don't get stuck on the specific numbers. What's important is the principles behind them. Tuition costs may rise, but the strategies in this book—graduate faster, save more money, and start earning sooner—will remain the same. Focus on these principles, and the numbers will take care of themselves.

4. **Assumptions Get Us Started, But Action Gets Us There:** This book utilizes estimates and assumptions. They are just starting points to give you a rough idea of costs and savings. To see what this book's strategies can do for you, enter your educational costs into the calculator on our website.

This Book's Assumptions

Here are the basic assumptions used in this book. Remember to plan based on your personal situation.

Credit Hours: Most schools require students to complete about 120 credit hours to graduate. We assume you need 126 credits to account for schools that require more. All schools have credit hour policies, so check your school's requirements before creating your college plan.

Cost Per Credit Hour/Semester: In this book, we used National Center for Education Statistics data to estimate school costs. However, you should check your school's costs when planning.

Transfer Credits: In this book, schools are assumed to accept all transfer credits. However, this is not always the case. Do your research and try to choose a college that accepts the transfer credits you have already earned or plan to earn.

Academic Performance: Another assumption is that you'll earn high enough grades to pass your courses and qualify to have your credits transferred and/or be able to take extra classes. If you're struggling academically, you'll need to work harder, get more support, or reduce your workload.

Course Availability: We assume that the courses you need to graduate early are available when you need to take them. If not, graduating may take longer. You could also get creative and take classes at another school or during summer break.

Salary Estimates: We used the National Association of Colleges and Employers 2022 Winter Survey data to estimate post-graduation income. However, salaries vary based on industry, location, and job market conditions.

Opportunity Costs: Assuming a degree is needed for your job, tuition is only part of the equation. Every extra year you are in college, you are losing out on income you could earn if you were in the workforce. This is why graduating faster can be such a big financial win.

Consider The Following

Credit Hours Needed/Cost Per Credit Hour: _____

Transfer Credits That Will Be Accepted: _____

Academic Performance Required for Credit Hour Overloading: _____

Career Ideas / Salary Estimates / Opportunity Costs: _____

_____

_____

_____

_____

Chapter 1: Is College Right for You?

Growing up, we heard a lot of advice about education. Go to college. Get good grades. Get a good job. It all sounded logical at the time, but something felt off. We knew there had to be more to it; after all, how many people follow that advice and end up stuck? Stuck in jobs they hate. Stuck with tons of student loan debt. Stuck helping someone else achieve their dreams while they ignore their own. None of us want to end up stuck, so it is time to ask ourselves a question almost no one is asking.

Is going to college the right choice for me, and if so, is there a better way to do it?

Look, people will have opinions. Everyone has something to say about college, including your parents, teachers, friends, and even strangers. But their advice comes from their own perspective, and you need to make the right choice for you. So ask yourself: *What do I really want out of life?* Warren Buffett's success shows why independent thinking is vital. He didn't build his fortune by doing what others told him. He followed his instincts, trusted his research, and made decisions aligned with his goals. The result? A net worth of over $100 billion. He didn't follow the crowd—he charted his own path to achieve incredible results. You can too. This book isn't just about how to excel in college and save money. It's about building a great life. That starts with doing what is right for you ASAP!

Asking the Right Questions: In high school, everyone asks, "Where are you going to college?" But there's a much more important question that most people never ask: *What do you want out of life?* College might be part of your path, but even if you attend college, it is only the beginning. In the big picture, the school you attend isn't as important as knowing your purpose in life. What's your dream? What kind of work excites you to get out of bed in the morning? What impact do you want to leave on the world? Learning those answers will help you find what you were put on this planet to do and help you make it happen.

3 Questions to Reflect on While Reading This Book

While reading this book, consider the following questions carefully. Let them guide you. After completing this book, you should be able to answer all of them confidently.

1. **Is college the right path to help me get what I want out of life?**

2. **If yes, how can I use the strategies in this book to graduate faster, save money, and reach my financial goals sooner?**

3. **What other options should I explore if college is not right for me?**

To Attend College or Not to Attend College: Perhaps you know your dream career and have done a ton of research on it. If that career requires a degree and pays enough to justify college. Great! That's a fantastic reason to go to college. Maybe you've got a full-ride scholarship, or your family can easily cover the cost of school. This is another case where pursuing college would be a great thing. However, for many people, choosing to go to college is just not that simple. Many young people are unsure of their future careers or how to pay for college. This book will help you make big decisions about college and your career. After all, you don't want to end up with a useless degree and a mountain of student loan debt. The truth is not everyone needs college. In fact, for some people, skipping college is the smarter choice. Many people without college degrees love their work and make six figures as electricians, plumbers, landscapers, entrepreneurs, and doing jobs you've never even heard of. At the same time, many college graduates are struggling to find jobs with halfway decent pay. In the end, it doesn't matter where your degree is from. What matters is finding a path you love that aligns with your goals and natural abilities.

Know Your Destination Before You Start Your Journey: Our stance is clear. No one should go to college without a plan. Every college student needs to know how they will pay for college, what degree they will earn, and how they will use their degree to repay their student loan debt and support themselves financially. Consider this: "39% of first-time college students seeking bachelor's degrees don't graduate."[1] Many students become dropouts because they lack the strategies and plan to navigate college successfully. Other students drop out because they realize college is not right for them. Unfortunately, when students drop out for either reason, they usually end up with student loan debt—but without a degree, that could help them earn more money to repay that debt. This is a tough spot to be in as a young person just getting started. A good number of students who do graduate also fail to plan. As a result, they stay in school longer than they should and rack up massive student debt balances. By staying in school longer, these students also miss out on earning income and valuable work experience. Another big problem is that many students don't think about how they will use their degrees to support themselves financially after graduation. When they try to use their degree to get a job, they are surprised that no jobs are available in their field or that the pay is miserably low. Often, these graduates can't pay their bills and are forced to move back in with their families and find other jobs they may not enjoy just to make ends meet. Considering the massive problems students face due to a lack of college planning, there is no question that a solution is needed. We wrote this book to be that solution. In the pages ahead, you can determine if college is right for you, learn how to prepare for college, confidently navigate challenges, and jumpstart your success.

---

[1] Hanson, M. (2024, August 16). *"College dropout rates."* EducationData.org.

The College Preparedness Checklist

Use this checklist to see if you're ready for the challenges of college. When you can check off every point, you'll be ready to begin your college journey, graduate, and start a rewarding career. This book's chapters will cover each checklist item in detail. So, every page you read will prepare you more for college. If you can't check all the boxes now, consider alternatives to college or improve your level of college preparedness.

CH 1: Is College Right for You? / CH 3: Choosing a Career

- **Academic Readiness:** You are prepared for college-level work.
- **Decision Clarity:** College will help you achieve your long-term personal and professional goals.
- **Career Clarity:** You have a plan for your future career. That career requires a college degree and justifies the cost of earning a degree.
- **Course of Study:** You have picked a major that aligns with your career goals.

CH 4: The Ultimate Education Game Plan / CH 5: Graduate Sooner & Save

- **Course Planning:** You have a plan for what courses to take and when.
- **Cost Awareness:** You understand how much college costs, how to graduate faster, and how to save money using the strategies in this book.

CH 6: Finding the Right College for You / CH 7: Applying and Getting Into College

- **College Selection:** You are applying to colleges that will help meet your academic, personal, and career-oriented goals.

CH 8,9,10: Paying for Your Education

- **Financial Strategy:** You have a plan to pay for college and repay any loans.

CH 11: Success in College and Life / CH 14: Life Skills to Help You Succeed

- **Habits, Work Ethic, and Life Skills:** You have developed the positive habits and life skills needed to succeed as an independent adult.
- **Goal-Oriented Time Management:** You are committed to focusing your time and energy on achieving your big goals and avoiding destructive behaviors.

CH 12: Financial Tips for College

- **Budgeting Plan:** You have a plan to budget and manage your finances.
- **Savings for Incidentals:** You have saved enough for incidental expenses.

CH 13: Mental and Physical Health

- **Physical and Mental Preparedness:** You are physically, mentally, and emotionally ready for the demands of college.
- **Health Management:** You have a plan to manage your physical and mental health while in college.

Chapter 1 Workbook

1. What Do You Want Out of Life?

Describe your ideal life in 10 years. What kind of work are you doing? How do you spend your time? Where do you live?

Career/Work:

_____

_____

_____

Lifestyle/Residence:

_____

_____

_____

2. Who Influences Your Thoughts on College?

List the people who have given you college advice (family members, teachers, friends). How do their opinions impact your decision?

Family:

_____

_____

Teachers:

_____

_____

Friends:

_____

_____

3. Is College the Right Path for You?

Do you think college is essential to achieving your long-term goals? Why or why not?

_____

_____

_____

_____

4. What Is Your Plan for Your Career and Course of Study?

What are your career goals, and how does your course of study help you achieve them?

_____

_____

_____

_____

_____

5. Non-College Path

If college isn't the best fit, what alternative path would you pursue, and how would you prepare for it?

_____

_____

_____

_____

_____

6. Personal Readiness: Based on the College Preparedness Checklist, what 3 areas are you strongest in? What 3 areas must you improve most to be ready for college? How will you continue building your strengths and improve your weak spots?

Strongest Areas

1: _____

2: _____

3: _____

Areas in Need of Improvement

1: _____

2: _____

3: _____

Chapter 2: Why Graduate in Under Four Years

Going to college is one of the most life-changing decisions you can make. But, even if you have chosen to go to college, how fast you graduate is also incredibly important. The less time you spend in school, the better your financial outcome. Staying in school longer will put you in a far worse financial position. You will have to pay way more for your education and lose out on both income and work experience. Most students don't realize just how much more it costs to take longer to graduate. The cost of an extra semester can be tens of thousands of dollars! Extra school bills and lost income can quickly add up to hundreds of thousands of dollars for students who stay in school a few years longer than they need to! Below is an example with fictional characters but very real costs to show you just how big the rewards are for graduating early.

The Tale of Two Paths: Ted vs. Frank

Two twins, Ted and Frank, had a choice. Which college to attend and how to complete their studies. They both chose to go to a nearby public college together and live at home with their family to save money. This was the most economical option they could find, with annual tuition costs averaging about $15,700 a year for full-time students. Compare this to the average annual cost of attending a private college, $33,600, or a not-for-profit college, $58,600.[2] They both majored in computer science and aimed for jobs paying $75,900 a year. However, they each took different graduation timelines.[3] Ted, who we'll call "Two-Year Ted," made a bold move. He compressed his entire college education into two years and did dual enrollment. Frank took the traditional path, earning his degree in four years—so he's "Four-Year Frank." Now, let's see how those decisions played out.

Career Progression: Ted graduated in just two years and immediately landed a job. Two years later, Ted is in a managerial role with higher pay. Employers love early graduates. They value their initiative and dedication, which make them great team members. Frank is still racking up debt while finishing school.

Financial Impact: By the time Frank got his first paycheck, Ted had already been paid over $150,000.

Student Loan Debt: Since Frank spent two more years in school, he owes about $26,000 more in student loan debt than Ted after counting interest. For the cost of their tuition, see Figure 6 for Frank and Figure 13 for Ted in Chapter 5. Frank pays $62,832. Ted pays $54,528.

---

[2] National Center for Education Statistics. (2024). "*Price of attending an undergraduate institution.*" Condition of Education. US Department of Education, Institute of Education Sciences.

[3] National Association of Colleges and Employers (NACE). (2022). "*Salary survey: Winter 2022.*" University of North Carolina Career Services.

Financial Difference: Due to differences in salary and debt, Ted is roughly $178,000 richer than Frank if we don't count taxes. Ted also has two more years of work experience and life to pursue his goals. By graduating early, Ted wins in four ways: he earns more, borrows less, climbs higher in his career, and reaches his goals faster.

Ted's 2-Year Path	**Frank's 4-Year Path**
▪ Missed salary because he graduated early: $0	▪ Missed potential salary for 2 years: $151,800
▪ Student loan and interest for 10 year payback at 6.53%: $83,724	▪ Student loan and interest for 10 year payback at 6.53%: $109,486
▪ **Total Cost: $83,724**	▪ **Total Cost: $261,286**

The Price of Not Graduating Early

Let's face it: Every semester you spend in school comes at a cost, not only in tuition and interest on student loans but also in lost earnings. Let's look at some estimates. They are from the National Association of Colleges and Employers 2022 salary survey. This survey estimates the salaries for recent college graduates and shows how much income you may lose out on by staying in school an extra year.

Figure 1			
Degree/Career	**2021 Salary Estimate**	**2022 Salary Estimate**	**% Change**
Humanities	$59,500	$50,681	— 14.8%
Communications	$58,174	$55,455	— 4.7%
Agriculture	$54,857	$57,807	+ 5.4%
Business	$58,869	$60,695	+ 3.1%
Social Sciences	$59,919	$61,173	+ 2.1%
Math & Sciences	$63,316	$66,760	+ 5.4%
Engineering	$71,088	$73,922	+ 4%
Computer Science	$72,173	$75,900	+ 5.2%
Reprinted from the 2022 Salary Survey with the permission of the National Association of Colleges and Employers, copyright holder.[4]			

---

[4] National Association of Colleges and Employers (NACE). (2022). "*Salary survey: Winter 2022.*" University of North Carolina Career Services.

How Hard Is It to Graduate Early? Cutting one or two semesters is very reasonable for hardworking students. Cutting one or more years is a very tough challenge. However, this is achievable if you're ambitious, dedicated, and your school allows it.

What If I Fail? Failure is only permanent if you quit. Let us say that again: Failure is only permanent if you quit. Aiming to graduate in two years but finishing in three, four, or even more? That's still a win. You're ahead of those who take longer or, worse, abandon their goals. The journey matters as much as the destination. Every semester brings you closer to graduation. Every challenge makes you stronger. Don't see delays or setbacks as failures—see them as opportunities to learn and grow.

What If You Succeed? Now, imagine you finish college in two years like "Ted" in the previous story. At twenty-two, you would have a net worth of approximately $100,000 to $200,000 higher than many of your peers. You'll have a head start paying off loans and saving money, which sets you up for even more future success. You can achieve all this before most of your classmates have even earned their first paycheck after college. Those extra years in the workforce will give you a huge edge, no matter your career path. Plus, if you're passionate about your career, why wait longer? Start pursuing your dreams now.

The Consequences of Dropping Out? Dropping out of college has long-lasting negative effects. Men without bachelor's degrees earn about $900,000 less on average during their working years than men with degrees. That's the harsh reality. For women, the gap is about $630,000.[5] Those are life-changing numbers that should motivate you to finish what you start. If you drop out, regret is likely to follow. In a study of one thousand college dropouts, over 70% regretted leaving school, and over 60% wished they could go back and finish.[6] Jim Rohn said it best: "Discipline weighs ounces. Regret weighs tons." It gets worse when you consider that about half of college dropouts have defaulted on their student loan payments.[7] Defaulting on loans will ruin your credit score. Destroying your credit limits your ability to rent an apartment, buy a car, or get a mortgage. Worst of all, student loans aren't wiped out by bankruptcy. If you don't pay them off or have them forgiven, you are stuck with them forever. Money can even be forcibly taken from you to start paying them back.

---

[5] Social Security Administration. "Research Summary: Education and Lifetime Earnings." (n.d.).

[6] Brown, M. (2017, November 2). "*College Dropouts and Student Debt.*" LendEDU.

[7] Ibid.

Chapter 2 Workbook

1. Fast-Tracking Your Future

Write a few sentences describing how you feel about the idea of graduating college early. Does it sound appealing? Why or why not?

_____

_____

_____

2. Comparing Ted vs. Frank

Compare the final outcome for Ted and Frank. What were 3 key differences, and what was the total impact?

Difference 1:

_____

Difference 2:

_____

Difference 3:

_____

Total Impact:

_____

3. The Importance of Experience

How would graduating early and having more work experience than your peers affect your job prospects and salary?

_____

_____

_____

4. What If You Succeed?

Think about the potential rewards of graduating in 2 to 3.5 years. How would graduating early affect your finances, career, and personal goals?

_____

_____

_____

Chapter 3: Choosing a Career

1. Work through the questions in this chapter.
2. Select and remove potential careers based on your answers.
3. Narrow it down to a few options and do a deep dive into the best ones.
4. Decide if you should pursue a degree or jump straight into work.
5. Make it happen!

Know Your Dream Career Before Starting College

Most people make the mistake of rushing into college before figuring out what they want to do with their lives. College should be about gaining the skills you need to improve your financial well-being and career prospects. But how can you do that if you don't know what career you're working toward and what you need to learn to be qualified? That's like starting a journey without knowing where you're headed. It's a fast way to end up lost in the dark and scary part of the woods. In contrast, knowing your destination can help you determine the quickest, easiest, and safest route to success. Even if you have already decided on a career, this chapter will help you further improve your plan, so don't skip it.

Self-Reflection Questions to Help You Find Your Dream Career: Choosing a career can be overwhelming, especially when you're unsure of your path. But the good news is you don't need all the answers right now. You just need to get started, and you will create a great plan over time. Use the following questions for inspiration.

What Makes You Happy?

What Are My Passions and Interests? What activities light you up? The things you enjoy doing can often point to fulfilling career ideas. You've got to love what you do. If you're not passionate about your work, success becomes an uphill battle.

What Did I Enjoy Doing as a Child? Reflect on the activities that brought you joy as a child. These early interests tell a lot about you and can explain your natural talents and career preferences.

What Do I Enjoy Doing in My Free Time? Hobbies aren't just for fun. They can show what tasks you enjoy in a career. You may even be able to make a career or side hustle out of them.

Do I Want Continuous Learning Opportunities? Some careers demand constant growth and learning. Those same careers often pay well because not everyone likes the challenge of constantly learning new skills.

Am I Willing to Take Risks? Certain careers require taking calculated risks. Are you comfortable with uncertainty and risk, or should you pick a more predictable job?

What Gives You an Edge? Finding Your Strengths

What Are My Strengths? Take an honest look at what you're good at. Ask people around you for feedback. It's more rewarding and fun to build on your strengths than to struggle in areas where you're weak.

What Types of Challenges Do I Enjoy? Do you prefer solving complex problems, or do you thrive with routine tasks? Knowing what challenges motivate you can help you choose the right career path.

What Work Environment Do I Thrive In? Are you more productive in a team or working solo? Do you thrive in a fast-paced environment or do you prefer more peace and quiet?

Questions to Align Your Education/Career with Your Life

What Lifestyle Do I Want? Your career will determine a lot about your lifestyle. Do you want long hours and frequent travel or more work-life balance?

What Are My Non-Negotiables? Identify your must-haves: salary, location, company culture, and growth opportunities. Knowing your non-negotiables will help you avoid career dissatisfaction and pass on jobs that won't serve you.

What Aligns with My Values? Values matter. Choose a company that aligns with your values. Examples of values are innovation, teamwork, and social responsibility. Because you're a hard worker, you'll likely prefer a company that rewards merit over seniority, offers ownership equity, and recognizes your effort. Also, consider working at a reputable company that respects employees, customers, and shareholders.

What Are My Long-Term Goals, and What Impact Do I Want to Make? Will the career you are considering help you achieve your goals?

Will This Career Allow Me to Make Enough Money to Obtain My Goals? What's the earning potential of your college major and desired career? If you're investing years of your life, ensure you will have a good payoff.

Job Market Demand: What's hot? What's not? Research which degrees and careers are in demand and pay well. After all, you don't want to graduate with a degree you can't use to support yourself financially.

Narrowing Down the Search – Research and Conversations

Have I Researched Different Industries and Roles? Research industries and jobs to find a niche that fits your skills and interests. See if the industries that interest you are growing or dying and what typical career paths look like.

Have I Talked to People in the Field? The best way to understand a career is to talk to professionals currently working in that field. Ask for advice, shadow them, or seek out internships. Many professionals want to help students. Good ways to reach them include networking with family, friends, alumni, LinkedIn, and local businesses. For example, Marshall got his first wealth management internship in high school through an introduction from a friend's parent. By observing and talking to professionals, you can better assess if a career suits you and if job prospects look strong or weak. If job prospects look weak, you may want to consider another path. Be grateful for all the help, and remember that building a network now can open important doors later.

Should It Be a Hobby or a Job? It's easy to get caught up in chasing a dream. When that happens, most people don't consider financial reality and end up disappointed. Passion is essential, but your path must also support your financial goals.

Let's look at a common dream that many people have: becoming a marine biologist. The idea of traveling the world and studying oceans is exciting. But here's the reality: The job often requires hard work, long hours writing papers, and a constant hunt for funding to keep research going. And let's talk about money. According to ZipRecruiter, the average salary for a marine biologist in 2025 was $43,396.[8] The average salary is down from $46,898 in 2024. Compare that to 2021 data from the US Bureau of Labor Statistics. Someone with a high school diploma will make about $42,081 yearly. In comparison, someone with a bachelor's degree in any field makes an average of $69,381 annually.[9] When you factor in a strenuous college education, college debt, unpaid internships, and the scarcity of jobs, many marine biology graduates find themselves financially worse off than people with no degree. We've seen this play out firsthand. Four of our friends, once passionate about marine biology, switched to different fields. And guess what? Now, they're making way more money in careers they enjoy even more. The best part? They can afford to travel to the most beautiful oceans in the world. For many people, art, marine biology, acting, or music should be hobbies, not careers. It's one thing to have a passion, but it's another to rely on that passion to put food on the table. Your passion is much more enjoyable when your next meal doesn't depend on it.

Marshall's dad, Lance Marshall Boen, is a successful artist. He's a rare exception to the typical starving artist. To Lance's knowledge, he is the only graduate from his Master of Fine Arts cohort who is still making a living as an artist. The rest? They had to switch careers to pay the bills. Lance recommends that anyone wanting to make a career from their passion should: (1) have a great business plan, (2) create high-quality, sellable work, and (3) have a strong work ethic and determination to persevere in tough times. Additionally, he recommends assessing whether your skills are good enough to do your passion professionally. The bottom line is you must find a way to balance what you love with a career that will give you the financial freedom to truly enjoy life.

---

[8] ZipRecruiter. (n.d.). "Salary: Marine biologist (January 2025) United States."
[9] US Bureau of Labor Statistics. (n.d.). "Education pays, 2021."

The Cost of Your Dream Life

Let's talk about something that's often overlooked but incredibly important: the lifestyle you want to live. It's easy to say, "I want to make a lot of money," but how much is "a lot"? And more importantly, how does that fit with the lifestyle you grew up with and the one you dream about? The first step is figuring out the numbers. How much money do you need to maintain the life you've known and the life you want? Most people never do this math, but it's crucial. Without knowing the financial gap between where you are and where you want to be, you're flying blind. Start by understanding the earning potential of the career you're choosing. Websites like Glassdoor and the Bureau of Labor Statistics provide accurate data. This data can help you set realistic expectations for your future.

Here's the reality check: If your upbringing was supported by a much higher income than your chosen career will provide, you'll face some tough choices. Maybe your parents each made $100,000-plus, but if your career choice averages less, you'll need to adjust your standard of living. This might mean you need to make financial sacrifices. Finding a major/career that aligns with your financial and personal goals is vital. It's not just about making money; it's about enjoying what you do and being able to support yourself while doing it. When your job matches your desired lifestyle and income, you'll be thriving, not just surviving. Take the time to figure out what you want out of life, both in terms of your career and the lifestyle it can provide. Because when you align your goals, work, and finances, you put yourself in a position to succeed on your terms.

Are You Well Suited to the Career Path?

The liberal arts system pushes for everyone to be good at everything. This idea is unrealistic and often harmful. It frustrates students and often makes them feel like failures. We have seen it firsthand, and you probably have, too.

Let us tell you a story. In 1940, George Reavis, superintendent of Cincinnati Public Schools, wrote a fable called "The Animal School." It's a powerful illustration of what's wrong with this "everyone must excel at everything" mindset. In the story, animals were forced to master swimming, climbing, running, and flying. Think about that. The fish, for example, was a great swimmer but a terrible runner and climber. The duck, which was a good swimmer, struggled with running. But, instead of improving its swimming skills, the duck wore out its webbed feet, trying to run better. The result? Ducky became just average at swimming. Then there's the eagle. He found a better way to climb. But he didn't follow the school's strict, unimaginative rules. So, he was punished and failed the class. Sound familiar? Most of us are like the animals in Reavis's story, with unique strengths and weaknesses. Sure, you have the rare standout who can do everything well. But for most of us, when the school system expects us to master everything, we inevitably fail at something, just like the fish when it tried running. If anyone keeps failing in a subject for years at a time, that feeling slowly crushes their self-esteem. Marshall, for instance, struggled in math, Spanish, and many other subjects, which made school a frustrating experience. School could have been more fun and productive for Marshall and many other students if they could have invested time in building their strengths rather than being fish trying to learn how to climb trees.

Now, let's talk about choosing a career path. The truth is, many jobs that require a degree don't even use most of what's taught in the classroom. But here's the catch—earning that degree is still necessary. Unfortunately, for now, that's the system we live in. Look carefully at what's required for the career you want. Does your chosen field require more than a bachelor's degree? Some jobs require more schooling, like becoming a doctor or lawyer. Are you capable of completing the educational requirements? If you're unsure about the requirements for your career, you need to do research. Then, consider whether you are willing and capable of spending more time and money in school. If not, pause and think. After all, you may burn out if the educational requirements to reach your goal are too high. That's why choosing a career that matches your strengths is so important. The lesson is simple: Success comes from aligning your goals with your strengths. That's how you avoid feeling like a fish trying to run. You'll face challenges—everyone does. But, when you play to your strengths, those challenges are just part of the process, not an unmovable roadblock.

Self-Assessment

As you consider college, rate your strengths and weaknesses on a scale from 0 to 10, where 0 represents weak and 10 represents strong. This will help you create a strategy based on your resources. It will also help you consider careers and courses of study that suit your strengths and downplay your weaknesses.

Academic Ability		Health Status		Financial Strength	
Math	/10	Physical Health	/10	Financial Strength	/10
English	/10	Mental Health	/10		
History	/10	Ambition	/10		
Science	/10	Time Management	/10		
Foreign Language	/10				

Acknowledging Strengths and Limitations: Recognizing your strengths and limitations is critical to achieving success in college and life. Not everyone excels in every area, and that's ok. The goal is to leverage your strengths, compensate for weaknesses, and plan accordingly. For example, higher grades in easier classes can partly offset lower grades in difficult ones. Or, if you struggle with time management, create stricter schedules and use tools like planners and reminders. If you have little money, be resourceful. Use the money-saving tips in this book to cut college costs. If you score low in certain classes, allocate more time and energy to those subjects. Similarly, if your physical or mental health needs attention, focus on improving those parts of yourself before diving into the stresses of college. Refer to later chapters on health management for guidance.

Becoming Future-Proof: 5 Winning Strategies

We live in a rapidly changing world. AI and automation are replacing more jobs every day. Global stability is stressed by wars and rapidly growing government debts. Use the following strategies to help secure your future.

Adaptability: Since life began, adaptability has been the key to success. With technology advancing rapidly, we must be able to quickly switch tasks, roles, and industries if needed.

Embrace Lifelong Learning and Develop High-Demand Skills: Knowing valuable skills makes you more desirable and difficult to replace. Continuously learn new skills that employers value. It will help keep you ahead of other people and machines. Focus on learning skills to solve society's biggest problems. As someone with Asperger's, Marshall cannot stress enough how critical people skills are. Communication and social-emotional skills are essential to success in school and beyond. In today's world, many young people lack emotional intelligence and communication abilities. By developing these skills, you will be far ahead of your peers.

Leverage AI to Enhance Your Work: Instead of fearing technology, learn how to use it to boost your productivity. For example, a lawyer using AI for non-billable tasks could save five hours weekly. They could then work five more billable hours at $500 per hour. That could add $10,000 a month, or $120,000 plus a year, to their income.

Choose Resilient Industries: Some fields, like health care, are essential. They offer more job security, no matter what happens with the economy.

"There is a saying that if you do what you love, you will never work a day in your life. At Apple, I learned that is a total crock. Rather, when you find a job you are passionate about, you will work hard, but you won't mind doing so. You will work harder than you ever thought possible, but the tools will feel light in your hands."

– Tim Cook, CEO of Apple

Chapter 3 Workbook

1. What Makes You Happy?

Think about your favorite activities. What are some things you enjoy doing in your free time? How could these activities translate into a career?

_____

_____

_____

_____

_____

2. What Are Your Strengths?

List your top strengths, skills, and talents. How could these strengths help you excel in certain careers?

_____

_____

_____

_____

_____

3. Types of Challenges

What types of challenges do you enjoy? Do you prefer solving complex problems? Or do you like routine tasks more? How could these preferences shape your career choices?

_____

_____

_____

4. Non-Negotiables

What are your career non-negotiables (e.g., salary, work location, company culture)? How do these influence the types of careers you might pursue?

_____

_____

_____

_____

_____

5. Networking with Professionals

Identify two professionals working in careers you're interested in. What questions will you ask them to learn more about the industry?

Professional #1:

1. _____
2. _____
3. _____

Professional #2:

1. _____
2. _____
3. _____

6. Balancing Passion with Financial Goals

Could your passion be better as a hobby than as a career? How will you balance doing what you love with financial stability?

_____

_____

_____

_____

_____

_____

7. Lifestyle Expectations

What kind of lifestyle do you want in the future? How much income do you need to support the lifestyle you desire?

_____

_____

_____

_____

_____

_____

_____

8. Are You Well Suited to This Career Path?

Review the educational requirements and skills needed for your chosen career. Are you confident that you can succeed in this path? Why or why not?

_____

_____

_____

_____

_____

_____

_____

_____

_____

_____

9. Preparing for Your Career

What steps do you need to take to reach your career goal? Consider required education, training, certifications, and work experience.

_____

_____

_____

_____

_____

_____

Notes:

_____

_____

_____

_____

_____

_____

Chapter 4: The Ultimate Education Game Plan

The sooner you begin planning for college, the more opportunities you'll have to save time and money. While this book can help students of all ages, many of the best ways to graduate early and save money are for high school students. If you're already in college, don't worry. After starting college, Marshall used just a few of the strategies in this book to graduate in two years and save a ton of money. If you are already in college, you can skip sections that apply to younger students. However, if you want to help younger family members or friends navigate college, consider reading all sections.

Building Relationships: Your Most Valuable Asset

Building strong relationships with your teachers and school staff is invaluable. If your goal is to graduate faster, you will need all the support you can get. You will also want to eliminate as much resistance as possible. Good relations with high school teachers and administrators will help you get easier access to AP classes, dual enrollment programs, and strong letters of recommendation. Strong relationships with college teachers and administrators will often help you get more transfer credits accepted. You may even get rules bent in your favor, have prerequisites waived, or be empowered to take more courses. Here's how to build relationships with school staff to achieve your goals while positively contributing to your school community.

1. **Engage Actively in Class:** Prove your dedication to learning. Ask questions, join discussions, and finish assignments on time. Active engagement signals that you care about your education.

2. **Support Your Peers:** Helping your classmates and improving the classroom will boost your reputation as a team player. Teachers value students who contribute to a collaborative and respectful atmosphere.

3. **Maintain Good Conduct Inside and Outside the Classroom:** Your behavior, inside and outside the classroom, influences how teachers and staff view you. Being responsible, respectful, and hardworking can encourage them to advocate for you.

4. **Show Persistence:** Persistence is key if you aim for more challenging courses or an accelerated educational path. You may face resistance from school admins who tell you to go easier on your studies. However, a good academic record, supportive parents, and clear goals can help you make your case for why you need to take hard classes.

5. **Communicate Clearly and Respectfully:** When facing objections to your academic plans, explain your reasoning thoughtfully and respectfully. Show the long-term benefits of your decisions. After advocating for yourself, you can also ask your parents for support if necessary. If you need help creating a plan or finding the best way to file an appeal, don't hesitate to ask the school administration for help. After all, when people start helping you,

they often become invested in your success. This can be a great way to get some school admins and teachers to support your ideas.

6. **Take Responsibility:** Teachers and administrators are more likely to support students who take responsibility for their mistakes and successes during their academic journey. Taking responsibility for your mistakes and not blaming others or external circumstances will make people more willing to help you succeed.

Writing Appeals to Graduate Early

If you want to take challenging courses or graduate early, which is the goal of this book, you may need to request permission to take extra credits or waive some requirements. Here's how to navigate the appeals process.

1. **Be Respectful and Clear:** Respectfully present your case. Explain why early graduation is important and how it aligns with your career goals.

2. **Provide Documentation:** To strengthen your appeal, include letters of support from professors or advisors that say you are up to the challenge. Requesting a meeting with the appeals committee can also give you a better opportunity to present your case.

3. **Persistence Is Key:** Don't give up if your appeal is denied. Refine your argument, gather more support, and try again and again. Persistence often pays off.

Step 1: Junior High – Laying the Foundation for Success

People think college prep starts in high school. Really, it begins in middle school, where you build the skills and habits for later academic success. Many students are told that middle school grades don't matter, which is not true. Just like Olympic athletes, top students begin developing their skills early. Middle school is the perfect time to focus on academics and forge a strong work ethic. The high school transition will be much easier if you've built good academic habits by eighth grade. If you don't work to develop your academic foundation early, higher-level classes may feel impossible.

Step 2: Consider High School Doesn't Have to Take 4 Years

Some highly motivated, capable students can graduate high school in under four years. While not all schools offer this option, many do. If this interests you and you're qualified, talk to your school's admin. Have these conversations as early as middle school or, at the very latest, at the beginning of high school. Graduating high school early can save a lot of time and money. You can start and finish college sooner and earn money from your career years before your peers. There are, of course, trade-offs. Expect an intense workload and less free time during the school year and summer.

Step 3: How to Get College Credit in High School

The following strategies will help you earn college credits while in high school, strengthen your college application, and save tons of time and money.

Dual Enrollment and Dual Credit: Earn College Credits in High School: Dual enrollment allows you to take college-level courses while still in high school. Some dual enrollment classes may also be dual credit. Dual credit lets you earn both high school and college credits simultaneously. To qualify, students must maintain a strong GPA to prove they can handle more demanding college courses. A grade of at least a B in dual enrollment classes is usually required to earn college credit. Many states have dual enrollment programs for high school students at community colleges. These courses often cost high school students little or nothing. Speak with your high school counselor about dual enrollment opportunities. Private or homeschooled students may face extra challenges and costs for dual enrollment. However, many states offer aid to help pay for dual enrollment classes. Remember to save all your transcripts, course descriptions, syllabi, and teacher contact information from the classes you take! You may need that information to get your transfer credits accepted at a university.

Advantages: Even if you have to pay the full cost for community college courses, dual enrollment can drastically reduce college costs because community college courses are almost always cheaper than four-year college credits. Marcus earned over 30 college credits during high school through dual enrollment for the cost of a few used textbooks. If you can do dual enrollment, take advantage of the program! It's a no-brainer!

Advanced Placement (AP) Courses: AP courses are rigorous high school classes that can lead to college credit if you score well on the AP exams and the college you ultimately attend accepts them. These courses are often weighted more heavily in your GPA. They can allow you to achieve up to a 5.0 compared to the standard 4.0 GPA. Whether you receive college credit and what type of credit you receive depends on your exam score and the college's policies. Scoring well on the AP exam (typically a 4 or 5) can earn you college credit. Some schools accept scores as low as 3, others will only accept scores of 5, and some may not grant credit for AP exams.

CLEP and DSST Exams: CLEP (College-Level Examination Program) and DSST (DANTES Subject Standardized Tests) may allow you to earn college credit or skip introductory classes by demonstrating your strength in various subjects. You can choose what subject(s) you want to take a test on, then study at your own pace online. Each exam costs about $100. You may also need to spend a little on study materials. Unlike AP exams, CLEP and DSST exams are available year-round and can be taken more than once. Check your intended college's credit policies before taking these exams. Most schools have minimum score requirements. Score requirements are often less strict than APs. Here's how schools handle your scores: Some won't give credit, but may let you skip general education courses. Others may give you elective credits or even credits for your degree. It all depends on the school, so know its policies before taking the test. If you are in the armed forces, a veteran, a spouse of someone in the armed forces, or work on a military base, you can often have the cost of a CLEP and DSST exam fully refunded by the US government.[10] As always, check your eligibility and specific rules for test cost refunds before starting.

Dual Enrollment and CLEP/DSST Exams vs. APs: If your college accepts them for credit, make taking dual enrollment and possibly CLEP and DSST exams part of your plan. They are better than AP classes. Here's why. It all comes down to time and results. Dual enrollment means you take real college courses while in high school and earn real college credits. There's no waiting around for an AP test at the end of the year, hoping you score high enough to get credit. You're getting credits right now, cutting down your time in college, and saving money on tuition. Now, let's talk about CLEP and DSST exams. These tests allow you to earn college credits by proving you know the material—it's as simple as that. Instead of a year in an AP class or a semester in college, you can self-study and take a test. If you score well, many schools will accept it for credit. Plus, you can take the tests as many times as you want. It's fast, efficient, and gets you ahead. The bottom line is that dual enrollment, CLEP, and DSST exams are faster and more flexible. They help you take control of your education and get ahead by cutting down your costs and time in college. However, APs can show colleges your academic skills, and they may be worth taking for that reason alone.

Step 4: Becoming Well Rounded

Good grades will help you succeed in school. But being well-rounded will help you succeed in life, which is what really matters. Everyone says being well-rounded is essential, but this phrase is so overused that it's lost its meaning. We saw classmates' parents aim to make their kids "well-rounded." So, they forced them to master a musical instrument, learn a foreign language, do sports, participate in clubs, and ace every test. If you are amazing enough to do that, we are impressed. But for most people, including us, trying to do all those things is impossible and sometimes harmful. A lot of smart people we know dropped out of college. They tried to master everything in school but could not handle the pressure of regular life. If so-called "well-rounded" students are struggling, perhaps we as a society have the wrong idea of what being well-rounded really means. We have thought long and hard about a better definition of well-rounded. The best answer we can give is that being well-rounded means someone has developed all the skill sets needed to succeed while facing adversity. This is a broad answer, so let's dig into it. First, you must understand and control your emotions. Use them to your benefit, not to your detriment. Second, you have all the life skills you need to succeed as an independent adult. Third, you have the courage, willpower, and grit to keep going and do what's right even when things get hard. You may fail again and again, but you do not give up trying to achieve the goals that matter most to you. Lastly, you continuously learn the knowledge required to achieve your goals. These skills

---

[10] College Board. (n.d.-a). "*CLEP military benefits.*" CLEP Military Benefits.

will take a lifetime to master, but if you start now, you will reach meaningful internal and external success far faster than the masses of people who never take the first step.

Step 5: Years One and Two of High School

As you step into high school, the stakes rise. Your grades during your first and second years of high school are a big deal. They will be on the transcripts you send to colleges. These early grades can significantly impact your future opportunities. Strong grades can boost your college applications. They can also make you eligible for merit-based scholarships. Depending on your academic capabilities, consider taking dual enrollment/credit, AP classes, and CLEP/DSST exams during the school year, summer, or both. Additionally, start saving as much money as you can for college.

Step 6: Years Three and Four of High School

Colleges will closely examine the grades you earn during your junior and senior years. Excelling academically is critical to getting into prestigious schools and obtaining scholarships. Check your future colleges' policies on dual enrollment, CLEP, DSST, and AP exams. After you know what credits will count toward your degree, earn as many as possible. If your high school lacks dual enrollment or AP options, consider summer courses at a community college. You could also prepare for CLEP/DSST exams to earn college credits. Continue saving money for college and following the steps from years one and two of high school.

ACT and SAT Preparation: While no longer required for all schools, high standardized test scores are incredibly helpful for earning merit-based scholarships and acceptance into college. Find out what score you need for your target schools and make a plan to work toward it. Practice timed tests regularly to get comfortable with the format and pace. Then, decide whether the SAT or ACT suits you better. The SAT is more about math and reading. The ACT is less math-focused, includes science, and is more time-pressured. If you're a student with learning differences, having an accommodation for extra time is a considerable benefit when taking either test. Most students score higher on their second try. So, take your first test early in your junior year. This gives you time for more practice and retakes. Some colleges will want your best score; others will consider all your scores. For this reason, make your best effort on every test you take. Also, if needed, secure academic accommodations and notify the exam proctor well before your test date. For more information on accommodations, see Chapter 15.

Marcus and Marshall's Paths: Marcus earned a full-ride to USC based on his SAT score of 1560, while Marshall increased his ACT score from 25 to 29 to unlock over $10,000 in merit-based scholarship opportunities.

Step 7: The Summer Before College

The summer before college is an amazing time to get ahead academically and financially. To earn college credits, you can take community college courses, CLEP/DSST exams, or even familiarize yourself with your future college by taking classes there. Taking classes at your future college in the summer may cost more, but it allows you to familiarize yourself with the campus, key facilities, and academic expectations. You also have the opportunity to meet professors and peers, creating valuable connections before the academic year begins. Furthermore, credits earned at your college are guaranteed to be counted for credit without any extra hassle. Staying engaged academically over the summer can benefit you. It will give you a head start on your college courses and keep you in school mode. All these factors come together to make the transition into college smoother. Furthermore, you can work over the summer to save money. Or even do an internship to gain experience, build your resume, and expand your network. This time is precious. Make the most of it and get off to a strong start on your journey toward college success.

Step 8: Starting College – How to Graduate Fast!

The beginning of your college career sets the stage for success. Work hard and pick up the pace as you get accustomed to your new school. If you take more credits than your tuition covers, consider earning credits through dual credit/enrollment with an online community college course. This is a great way to save money because most remote community college courses are more cost-effective and easier than university classes.

Using RateMyProfessors.com to Find Great Teachers and Avoid Bad Ones

RateMyProfessors.com is a powerful tool for improving your college experience. The website features student reviews of professors based on their teaching style, workload, and communication abilities. Strategically choosing professors will ensure a more fun and successful college experience. Here's how to use this tool.

- **Use the Search Feature:** First, try to look up teachers by name. If this does not work or you want information about all your school's teachers, look up your school and search by department.

- **Find Great Teachers:** Look for professors who are praised for their communication, feedback, and ability to motivate students to succeed. These professors will enhance your learning and make classes more engaging.

- **Avoid Bad Professors:** Steer clear of those frequently described as unhelpful, disorganized, lazy, or disrespectful. They can make your journey harder, especially if you already have a heavy workload.

- **Don't Always Choose the Easy Grade:** While tempting, easy A's won't always help you grow. Professors who challenge you will better prepare you for your future coursework and career.

- **Match Your Learning Style:** Use reviews to find professors whose teaching style fits your learning preferences.

- **Avoid Busy Work:** If you are juggling multiple courses, avoid professors who pile on busy work. Instead, look for those who focus on meaningful assignments.

- **Focus on Communication:** Professors who give clear instructions and helpful feedback will help you achieve far more academic success. Avoid professors who are bad communicators. Their unclear instructions will reduce your learning and cause you to be poorly prepared and score lower on tests and assignments.

- **Beware of Extremes:** Don't rely on overly positive or negative reviews. Prioritize reliable feedback from students who performed well.

- **Ask Upperclassmen:** Online reviews aren't everything. Seek advice from older students to get a clearer picture of professors.

- **Write Reviews:** Teachers and future students will likely read them. Be respectful, honest, and helpful. Give constructive criticism and praise where appropriate. Do the same for teachers' course evaluations. Their jobs often depend on reviews.

Transferring College Credits: A Key to Saving Time and Money

The transfer process may seem complex. But it's a common and critical part of many students' educational paths. Students often transfer high school credits to college, move from a community college to a four-year school, switch universities, or return to school after time off. The next section will show you how to transfer credits to earn your degree faster and at a lower cost.

Why Transfer College Credits?

Save Time and Money: Transferring credits allows you to avoid retaking courses you've already completed. It's the most effective way to reduce the total cost, time, and effort of earning your degree.

Flexibility: Transferring credits allows you to switch schools for any reason while retaining some or all of your progress.

Access to Better Programs: Starting at a community college or a less competitive university can be a strategic way to save money and transfer to a more prestigious institution later. In some states, like California, if you meet GPA and credit requirements at a community college, there are guaranteed paths to transfer your credits to get accepted into more competitive state schools.[11]

Maximizing Transfer Credits and Class Scheduling

1. **Prioritize Prerequisites:** Take prerequisite courses as soon as possible. They are typically necessary for moving on to advanced coursework, and not having prerequisite courses finished can push back your graduation timeline. Also, schools usually accept transfer credits for general and elective courses but not for major-specific classes. For this reason, only take major-specific courses at your primary college unless you are sure credits earned elsewhere will be accepted.

2. **Register Early and Plan Around Rarely Offered Classes:** Some courses are only available during specific semesters or times of day. Take them ASAP to avoid delays. Rarely offered classes and courses taught by great professors usually fill up fast. We can't stress enough the importance of early registration. It gets you the best teachers, class times, and chances of meeting your scheduling needs.

3. **Dual Enrollment/Dual Credit in College:** Dual enrollment, in this case, means you take a few online courses at a community college while attending your main university. Dual credit means you'll transfer those community college courses to count toward your university degree. This strategy can reduce tuition costs if you are taking more than the number of credit hours covered by tuition at your primary college. This is because community college courses are almost always cheaper per credit hour.

4. **Bypassing Hard Classes:** Community college courses are almost always easier than their four-year counterparts. If you anticipate struggling with a course, consider taking it online through a community college.

5. **Exceeding Credit Limits:** If your university limits the number of credits you can take per semester, enrolling in additional community college courses can sometimes be a loophole. At least, it was in Marshall's experience.

Understanding the Credit Transfer Process

1. **Accreditation Matters:** Ensure your current institution is regionally accredited. Most colleges only accept transfer credits from accredited institutions. You can verify accreditation through the US Department of Education or the Council for Higher Education Accreditation

2. **Timing and Deadlines:** Transfer processes take time, and deadlines vary by school. Request official transcripts from every institution you've attended. Ensure they are sent directly to the new school as soon as possible. Your current and prospective schools have advisors who can help you navigate the credit transfer process and clarify which credits will be accepted.

---

[11] University of California. (n.d.). *"Transfer admission guarantee (TAG)."* Transfer Admission Guarantee (TAG).

3. **Contact Admissions:** This step can prevent you from wasting time and money earning credits that don't count toward your degree! Always contact your college's admissions or academic advising office to get a written confirmation of their policies for accepting transfer credits from them or their website and save it. If a college changes policies and you need to appeal to get your transfer credits accepted, having that written document can help support your case and allow your credits to be grandfathered in. Most colleges cap the number of transfer credits between 30 and 60-plus. The number of core or major-specific courses that can be transferred is usually lower than the total number of credits that can be transferred. However, every college has different rules for accepting AP, CLEP/DSST exams, dual enrollment, and community college credits. Admissions will give you specific details about how your credits will transfer and how they'll apply to your degree. Be prepared to provide course syllabi, descriptions, and additional course information. Do your best to attend a school that accepts your hard-earned credits.

4. **Course Equivalency Guides and Transfer Tools:** Many schools provide guides showing how courses from other institutions transfer. These guides are usually on the school's website or at the academic advising office. Websites like Transferology are also great for checking how credits will transfer between institutions. As mentioned before, many states offer structured transfer pathways called Transfer Admission Guarantee (TAG) programs, making transferring from two-year to four-year in-state institutions easier. Below is California's program for reference.

UC TAG Program: This program guarantees admission to specific UC campuses for students meeting GPA and course requirements at California community colleges.

California State University Associate Degree for Transfer (ADT): This program streamlines the transfer process from California community colleges to California State schools.

5. **Appeal Credit Decisions:** If certain credits are not accepted, ask about the appeals process. If necessary, provide additional documentation or explanations.

6. **Plan Your Coursework:** Once your credits are transferred, work with an advisor to map out the remainder of your degree. This will help you save money by avoiding unnecessary classes and graduating early or on time.

How Much Money You Can Save With These Strategies

If you're wondering how much you can save using the strategies in this chapter, wait no longer. For community college courses, we assume you'll pay the full cost of $260 per credit hour. However, taking dual enrollment courses through your high school may be free or low-cost. This could save you hundreds or thousands of dollars beyond what's calculated here. For AP, CLEP, or DSST exams, we estimate a total cost of $200. This includes $100 for the exam and $100 for study materials and transportation to the test center. If you score high enough to bypass a 3-credit course, you'll save three times the college's per-credit-hour rate.

Figure 2			
Cost Savings by College Type	**4-Year Public**	**4-Year Private For-Profit**	**4-Year Private Not-for-Profit**
Cost Per Credit Hour	$476	$767	$932
Savings Per Credit Hour Done at a Community College	$476−$260 = $216	$767−$260 = $507	$932−$260 = $672
Savings For Each 3-Credit Community College/Dual Enrollment Course	$216 x 3 = $648	$507 x 3 = $1,521	$672 x 3 = $2,016
Savings For Each AP, CLEP, or DSST Exam Transferred Assuming 3 Credit Hours Earned	($476 x 3) − $200 = $1,228	($767 x 3) − $200 = $2,101	($932 x 3) − $200 = $2,596
Savings From Transferring 32 Credits From a Community College	$216 x 32 = $6,912	$507 x 32 = $16,224	$672 x 32 = $21,504
Transfer 32 Credit Hours and Work a Year Sooner. Salary Ranging from $50,681 to $75,900	**Low End:** $50,681 + $6,912 = $57,593 **High End:** $75,900 + $6,912 = $82,812	**Low End:** $50,681 + $16,224 = $66,905 **High End:** $75,900 + $16,224 = $92,124	**Low End:** $50,681 + $21,504 = $72,185 **High End:** $75,900 + $21,504 = $97,404

Chapter 4 Workbook

1. Becoming a Great Student

How will you show active engagement in your classes and build a positive reputation with your teachers and administrators?

_____

_____

_____

_____

_____

2. Communicating Your Goals

If you plan to take challenging courses or graduate early, how will you clearly and respectfully communicate your academic goals to your school administration? Also, what will you do if your initial plan is denied and you must file an appeal?

_____

_____

_____

_____

_____

3. Graduating High School Early

Would you be able to graduate high school in fewer than four years? Why or why not? Consider the trade-offs involved in this decision.

_____

_____

_____

_____

4. Dual Enrollment vs. AP Courses

Compare dual enrollment and AP courses. Which option do you think would benefit you more, and why?

_____

_____

_____

5. CLEP and DSST Exams

If CLEP or DSST exams work for you, what subjects would you like to take a test for? How much time and money would this save you in college?

_____

_____

_____

6. Preparing for Standardized Tests

Which standardized test (ACT or SAT) best fits your strengths? What is your strategy for preparing and improving your scores?

_____

_____

_____

7. Maximizing Transfer Credits

If you plan to transfer college credits, what will you do to ensure your credits are accepted at your chosen school? Why is this important for saving time and money?

_____

_____

_____

8. Using RateMyProfessors.com

How will you use RateMyProfessors.com to choose better teachers? Why is finding the right professor important for your academic success?

_____

_____

_____

9. Calculating Your Savings

Using the strategies in this chapter that would be best for you, estimate your potential savings with the easy-to-use calculator on our website.

_____

_____

_____

_____

Chapter 5: How to Graduate Sooner and Save

College costs can feel overwhelming, but with thoughtful planning, you can slash the price tag on your degree. In this chapter, we'll break down the real cost of college by type of school, compare graduation timelines, and build off the last chapter's strategies to help you save tens of thousands to potentially over $100,000.

Understanding the Average Costs of School Attendance

Calculating average college costs provides an excellent baseline for making financial decisions. However, the numbers below are just averages. Your costs could be higher or lower depending on factors like location and type of school. Also, college costs may rise over time. So, if applicable, adjust the numbers in this book for annual tuition increases when planning for college.

The calculations in the pages ahead will cover in-person schools that operate on the semester system, charge a set price for full-time students, and additional fees for credit hours above and beyond those included in base tuition. To find cost calculations for online colleges, schools that charge per credit hour, and colleges that are on a quarter or trimester system go to our website AtlasClass.com.

Tip: Our online college cost calculators have a feature where you can input the costs of different schools you are considering so you can compare options. If you are still deciding what type of school to attend, this chapter will give you a general idea of how much different types of schools and graduation timelines cost.

Graduating College: Slow to Fast: There are many ways to complete a bachelor's degree. You can take the traditional four-year path. Or, you could use accelerated methods to graduate in as little as two years. The pages ahead show a breakdown of graduation timelines, from the slowest (six years) to the fastest (two years). The longer you take to graduate, the more your degree will cost. This is due to more tuition costs, school fees, living costs, and lost earnings from not working full-time. Alternatively, the faster you graduate, the less school will cost, and the sooner you can reach financial success.

A Final Reason to Graduate Early – Rapidly Rising College Costs

A US News survey found that, from 2002 to 2023, private, public, and out-of-state college tuition rose by between 134% and 175%. For example, if a $10,000 tuition increases by 3% annually, it will cost you $300 more each year you are in school. Graduating early will save you hundreds to thousands of dollars by avoiding annual price increases. To keep it simple, we did not include inflation in our calculations. So, your savings from graduating early would likely be larger than our calculations show.

Assumptions for Cost Calculations

1. **Taking More Credit Hours Than Normal:** Many schools allow students to take up to 18 credit hours per semester for the price of standard tuition. We assume students can take more than 18 credits per semester (credit hour overloading) and pay for the extra credits earned at their primary college or through dual enrollment at a community college.

2. **Total Credit Hours:** We assume students need 126 credits to graduate. It's more than the standard 120 credits to account for schools that require more. If your school requires fewer than 126 credits, you should be able to graduate faster and spend less than the calculations show.

3. **Being Able to Transfer Credits Into Your College:** For some examples below, we assume that all your outside credits will transfer and that a school will accept a certain number of those credits. Every school is different, so research credit acceptance policies and plan accordingly.

Level and Control of Institution	Off-Campus Living with Family	On Campus	Off-Campus Not Living with Family	Net Cost Per Credit Hour
Figure 3: Average cost by school type and living situation based on data from the National Center for Education.				
2-Year Schools				
In-State Public	$10,199	$16,641	$20,910	$260
4-Year Schools				
In-State Public	$15,708	$27,146	$27,756	$476
Private for Profit	$23,885	$33,574	$34,071	$767
Private Nonprofit	$46,280	$58,628	$57,519	$932
The average total cost of attending degree-granting institutions for first-time, full-time degree/certificate-seeking undergraduate students, by level and control of institution and student living arrangement: The academic year 2022–23 and the average net cost per credit hour after aid 2020–2021.[12][13][14]				

[12] National Center for Education Statistics. (2024). *"Price of Attending an Undergraduate Institution."* US Department of Education, Institute of Education Sciences.

[13] BestColleges. (2024). *College cost per credit hour: How to calculate and reduce your expenses.*

[14] National Center for Education Statistics. (2024). *Price of attending an undergraduate institution* (Table 331.30). U.S. Department of Education, Institute of Education Sciences.

6-Year Bachelor's Degree Graduation – Slowest and Highest Cost

Plan: Take 12 credits per semester for twelve semesters = 144 total credits.

Common Scenarios: Failure to pass classes, changing majors, adding minors, or working long hours while in school.

Consequences: Significantly higher cost and delayed entry into the workforce.

Figure 4			
Living Situation	**In-State Public**	**Private For-Profit**	**Private Nonprofit**
Off-Campus	$15,708 x 6 = $94,248	$23,885 x 6 = $143,310	$46,280 x 6 = $277,680
Off-Campus	$27,146 x 6 = $162,876	$33,574 x 6 = $201,444	$58,628 x 6 = $351,768
Off-Campus	$27,756 x 6 = $166,536	$34,071 x 6 = $204,426	$57,519 x 6 = $345,114
Cost Increase for 6-Year Graduation Compared to 4-Year Graduation			
Average Increase	**$47,073**	**$61,020**	**$108,285**
Off-Campus	$94,248 − $62,832 = $31,416	$143,310 − $95,540 = $47,770	$277,680 − $185,120 = $92,560
Off-Campus	$162,876 − $108,584 = $54,292	$201,444 − $134,296 = $67,148	$351,768 − $234,512 = $117,256
Off-Campus	$166,536 − $111,024 = $55,512	$204,426 − $136,284 = $68,142	$345,114 − $230,076 = $115,038

5-Year Bachelor's Degree Graduation

Plan: Take 12–13 credits per semester for ten semesters = 120–130 total credits.

Common Scenarios: Balancing work and school or academic challenges.

Figure 5			
Living Situation	**In-State Public**	**Private For-Profit**	**Private Nonprofit**
Living with Family	$15,708 x 5 = $78,540	$23,885 x 5 = $119,425	$46,280 x 5 = $231,400
On-Campus	$27,146 x 5 = $135,730	$33,574 x 5 = $167,870	$58,628 x 5 = $293,140
Off-Campus	$27,756 x 5 = $138,780	$34,071 x 5 = $170,355	$57,519 x 5 = $287,595
Cost Increase for 5-Year Graduation Compared to 4-Year Graduation			
Average Increase	**$23,537**	**$30,510**	**$54,142**
Living with Family	$78,540 − $62,832 = $15,708	$119,425 − $95,540 = $23,885	$231,400 − $185,120 = $46,280
On-Campus	$135,730 − $108,584 = $27,146	$167,870 − $134,296 = $33,574	$293,140 − $234,512 = $58,628
Off-Campus	$138,780 − $111,024 = $27,756	$170,355 − $136,284 = $34,071	$287,595 − $230,076 = $57,519

4-Year Bachelor's Degree Graduation – Standard Path

Plan: Take 15–16 credits per semester for eight semesters = 120–128 total credits.

Figure 6			
Living Situation	**In-State Public**	**Private For-Profit**	**Private Nonprofit**
Living with Family	$15,708 x 4 = $62,832	$23,885 x 4 = $95,540	$46,280 x 4 = $185,120
On-Campus	$27,146 x 4 = $108,584	$33,574 x 4 = $134,296	$58,628 x 4 = $234,512
Off-Campus	$27,756 x 4 = $111,024	$34,071 x 4 = $136,284	$57,519 x 4 = $230,076

3.5-Year Bachelor's Degree Graduation (Accelerated Path)

Plan: Take 18 credits per semester for seven semesters = 126 credits.

Time Frame: One semester shorter than the standard 4-year plan.

Workload: The 3.5-year timeline is a great option. It lets students finish a degree faster while still enjoying a standard college experience. Taking 18 credit hours per semester is challenging but manageable with a solid work ethic and a good academic skill set.

Figure 7			
3.5-Year Bachelor's Degree Graduation			
Living Situation	**In-State Public**	**Private For-Profit**	**Private Nonprofit**
Living with Family	$15,708 x 3.5 = $54,978	$23,885 x 3.5 = $83,598	$46,280 x 3.5 = $161,980
On-Campus	$27,146 x 3.5 = $95,011	$33,574 x 3.5 = $117,509	$58,628 x 3.5 = $205,198
Off-Campus	$27,756 x 3.5 = $97,146	$34,071 x 3.5 = $119,249	$57,519 x 3.5 = $201,317
3.5-Year Graduation Savings Compared to 4-Year Graduation			
Average Savings	**$11,768**	**$15,255**	**$27,071**
Living with Family	$62,832 − $54,978 = $7,854	$95,540 − $83,598 = $11,942	$185,120 − $161,980 = $23,140
On-Campus	$108,584 − $95,011 = $13,573	$134,296 − $117,509 = $16,787	$234,512 − $205,198 = $29,314
Off-Campus	$111,024 − $97,146 = $13,878	$136,284 − $119,249 = $17,035	$230,076 − $201,317 = $28,759

3-Year Graduation

To make this awesome plan a reality, you'll need a heavier course load, which may include transfer credits or dual enrollment. You can decide if you want to load up on courses during regular semesters and keep summers/breaks free. Alternatively, you can take fewer classes per semester and take classes over break periods if your school offers them. General education and elective courses are often offered over break periods. Higher-level courses may only be available during the school year.

3-Year Graduation Primary College Only

Plan: Take 18 credits per semester for six semesters (108 credits) and 18 extra credits during summer and/or break periods if your school offers the necessary classes at those times. Or, you could take 21 credits per semester and have breaks off.

Potential Challenges: Heavy workload, and some schools may limit credits per semester or charge additional fees.

Time Flexibility: Taking 21 credits per semester would mean more work but freedom over breaks and summer to have fun and work to save money for college.

Figure 8			
3-Year Graduation Primary College Only (No Dual Enrollment)			
Living Situation	**In-State Public**	**Private For-Profit**	**Private Nonprofit**
Living with Family	($15,708 x 3) + ($476 x 18) = $55,692	($23,885 x 3) + ($767 x 18) = $85,461	($46,280 x 3) + ($932 x 18) = $155,616
On-Campus	($27,146 x 3) + ($476 x 18) = $90,006	($33,574 x 3) + ($767 x 18) = $114,528	($58,628 x 3) + ($932 x 18) = $192,660
Off-Campus	($27,756 x 3) + ($476 x 18) = $91,836	($34,071 x 3) + ($767 x 18) = $116,019	($57,519 x 3) + ($932 x 18) = $189,333
3-Year Graduation Savings Compared to 4-Year Graduation			
Average Savings	**$14,969**	**$16,704**	**$37,366**
Living with Family	$62,832 − $55,692 = $7,140	$95,540 − $85,461 = $10,079	$185,120 − $155,616 = $29,504
On-Campus	$108,584 − $90,006 = $18,578	$134,296 − $114,528 = $19,768	$234,512 − $192,660 = $41,852
Off-Campus	$111,024 − $91,836 = $19,188	$136,284 − $116,019 = $20,265	$230,076 − $189,333 = $40,743

Graduate in 3-Years with Dual Enrollment

Plan: Take 18 credits per semester for six semesters = 108 credits. Plus, 6 additional credits from your primary college and 12 credits from a community college for a total of 126 credits. By taking 12 lower-cost credits from a community college, you save more money than taking all your classes at your primary college.

Figure 9			
3-Year Graduation Primary College + Dual Enrollment			
Living Situation	**In-State Public**	**Private For-Profit**	**Private Nonprofit**
Living with Family	($15,708 x 3) + ($476 x 6) + ($260 x 12) = $53,100	($23,885 x 3) + ($767 x 6) + ($260 x 12) = $79,377	($46,280 x 3) + ($932 x 6) + ($260 x 12) = $147,552
On-Campus	($27,146 x 3) + ($476 x 6) + ($260 x 12) = $87,414	($33,574 x 3) + ($767 x 6) + ($260 x 12) = $108,444	($58,628 x 3) + ($932 x 6) + ($260 x 12) = $184,596
Off-Campus	($27,756 x 3) + ($476 x 6) + ($260 x 12) = $89,244	($34,071 x 3) + ($767 x 6) + ($260 x 12) = $109,935	($57,519 x 3) + ($932 x 6) + ($260 x 12) = $181,269
3-Year Dual Enrollment Graduation Savings Compared to 4-Year Graduation			
Average Savings	**$17,561**	**$22,788**	**$45,430**
Living with Family	$62,832 − $53,100 = $9,732	$95,540 − $79,377 = $16,163	$185,120 − $147,552 = $37,568
On-Campus	$108,584 − $87,414 = $21,170	$134,296 − $108,444 = $25,852	$234,512 − $184,596 = $49,916
Off-Campus	$111,024 − $89,244 = $21,780	$136,284 − $109,935 = $26,349	$230,076 − $181,269 = $48,807
Average Additional Savings Doing 12 Credit Hours of Dual Enrollment			
Public: ($476 x 12) − ($260 x 12) = $2,592			
Private for Profit: ($767 x 12) − ($260 x 12) = $6,084			
Private Not for Profit: ($932 x 12) − ($260 x 12) = $8,064			

Graduating in 2.5 Years: All Classes at Your Primary College

Plan: You must plan your coursework carefully, ensuring you take prerequisites as early as possible to avoid bottlenecks. To graduate in 2.5 years, you'll need to take 25–26 credits per semester. Or you could spread it out by taking 20–21 credits per semester and 24 total credits during summer and winter breaks. Take 18 credits per semester for five semesters = 90 credits included in the cost of tuition. Plus, 36 additional paid credits from your primary college.

Failure Risk/GPA Requirements: There is little room for error. Failing a class could hurt your chances of graduating in 2.5 years. Schools may also require a high GPA to approve credit overloading beyond 18 credits.

Financial Aid: If your aid or loans don't cover the extra credits, you may need to pay out of pocket.

Work-Life Balance: A heavy course load will leave less time for extracurriculars, work, or relaxation.

Figure 10			
2.5-Year Graduation Primary College Only			
Living Situation	**In-State Public**	**Private For-Profit**	**Private Nonprofit**
Living with Family	($15,708 x 2.5) + ($476 x 36) = $56,406	($23,885 x 2.5) + ($767 x 36) = $87,325	($46,280 x 2.5) + ($932 x 36) = $149,252
On-Campus	($27,146 x 2.5) + ($476 x 36) = $85,001	($33,574 x 2.5) + ($767 x 36) = $111,547	($58,628 x 2.5) + ($932 x 36) = $180,122
Off-Campus	($27,756 x 2.5) + ($476 x 36) = $86,526	($34,071 x 2.5) + ($767 x 36) = $112,790	($57,519 x 2.5) + ($932 x 36) = $177,350
2.5-Year Graduation Savings Compared to 4-Year Graduation			
Average Savings	**$18,169**	**$18,153**	**$47,661**
Living with Family	$62,832 − $56,406 = $6,426	$95,540 − $87,325 = $8,215	$185,120 − $149,252 = $35,868
On-Campus	$108,584 − $85,001 = $23,583	$134,296 − $111,547 = $22,749	$234,512 − $180,122 = $54,390
Off-Campus	$111,024 − $86,526 = $24,498	$136,284 − $112,790 = $23,494	$230,076 − $177,350 = $52,726

Graduating in 2.5 Years (Dual Enrollment):

Plan: Take 18 credits per semester for five semesters (90 credits), plus pay for an additional 24 credits at your primary college and 12 at a community college.

Figure 11			
2.5-Year Graduation (Dual Enrollment)			
Living Situation	**In-State Public**	**Private For-Profit**	**Private Nonprofit**
Living with Family	($15,708 x 2.5) + ($476 x 24) + ($260 x 12) = $53,814	($23,885 x 2.5) + ($767 x 24) + ($260 x 12) = $81,241	($46,280 x 2.5) + ($932 x 24) + ($260 x 12) = $141,188
On-Campus	($27,146 x 2.5) + ($476 x 24) + ($260 x 12) = $82,409	($33,574 x 2.5) + ($767 x 24) + ($260 x 12) = $105,463	($58,628 x 2.5) + ($932 x 24) + ($260 x 12) = $172,058
Off-Campus	($27,756 x 2.5) + ($476 x 24) + ($260 x 12) = $83,934	($34,071 x 2.5) + ($767 x 24) + ($260 x 12) = $106,706	($57,519 x 2.5) + ($932 x 24) + ($260 x 12) = $169,286
2.5-Year Dual Enrollment Graduation Savings Compared to 4-Year Graduation			
Average Savings	**$20,761**	**$24,237**	**$55,725**
Living with Family	$62,832 − $53,814 = $9,018	$95,540 − $81,241 = $14,299	$185,120 − $141,188 = $43,932
On-Campus	$108,584 − $82,409 = $26,175	$134,296 − $105,463 = $28,833	$234,512 − $172,058 = $62,454
Off-Campus	$111,024 − $83,934 = $27,090	$136,284 − $106,706 = $29,578	$230,076 − $169,286 = $60,790

Graduating in 2 Years

Graduating in two years is an ambitious and challenging goal. This path may not be possible at all schools or for all majors. Many universities have strict policies on course loads, the sequence of prerequisite courses, and limits on how many credits you can take per semester. Schools may also restrict the number of transfer credits from other institutions. These factors make this goal challenging, but it is still often possible.

Plan: Take 18 credits per semester for four semesters (72 credits), plus pay for another 54 credits at your primary college.

Figure 12			
2-Year Graduation Primary College Only			
Living Situation	**In-State Public**	**Private For-Profit**	**Private Nonprofit**
Living with Family	($15,708 x 2) + ($476 x 54) = $57,120	($23,885 x 2) + ($767 x 54) = $89,188	($46,280 x 2) + ($932 x 54) = $142,888
On-Campus	($27,146 x 2) + ($476 x 54) = $79,996	($33,574 x 2) + ($767 x 54) = $108,566	($58,628 x 2) + ($932 x 54) = $167,584
Off-Campus	($27,756 x 2) + ($476 x 54) = $81,216	($34,071 x 2) + ($767 x 54) = $109,560	($57,519 x 2) + ($932 x 54) = $165,366
2 Year Graduation Savings Compared to 4-Year Graduation			
Average Savings	**$21,369**	**$19,602**	**$57,957**
Living with Family	$62,832 − $57,120 = $5,712	$95,540 − $89,188 = $6,352	$185,120 − $142,888 = $42,232
On-Campus	$108,584 − $79,996 = $28,588	$134,296 − $108,566 = $25,730	$234,512 − $167,584 = $66,928
Off-Campus	$111,024 − $81,216 = $29,808	$136,284 − $109,560 = $26,724	$230,076 − $165,366 = $64,710

Graduate in 2 Years Dual Enrollment (What Marshall Did)

Marshall's strategy was to take as many classes as possible each semester and over summer and winter breaks to graduate in two years. For many semesters, he took as many as 27 credit hours. This approach saved time and money, though it required meticulous planning and a strong GPA to get approval for such a heavy load.

1. **Maximize Credit Load:** Marshall took all 18 credit hours covered by the price of tuition each semester. He also got approval to take extra classes, which he did.

2. **Use Community College Courses:** For most semesters, he took one community college course for dual credit in addition to his other classes. The courses were less expensive and easier academically.

3. **Take Classes Year-Round:** Marshall kept a fast academic pace. He took courses during the academic year and winter, spring, and summer breaks.

4. **Strong GPA:** Marshall maintained a high GPA to be allowed to overload classes.

5. **Close Proximity to Campus:** Living on campus during his first year and being nearby for his second allowed him to save time, money, and energy on transportation.

Total Education Cost Formula: Total cost = 2 years in school + 42 credits at primary university not covered by tuition + 12 lower-cost community college credits.

Figure 13			
2-Year Graduation Dual Enrollment			
Living Situation	**In-State Public**	**Private For-Profit**	**Private Nonprofit**
Living with Family	($15,708 x 2) + ($476 x 42) + ($260 x 12) = $54,528	($23,885 x 2) + ($767 x 42) + ($260 x 12) = $83,104	($46,280 x 2) + ($932 x 42) + ($260 x 12) = $134,824
On-Campus	($27,146 x 2) + ($476 x 42) + ($260 x 12) = $77,404	($33,574 x 2) + ($767 x 42) + ($260 x 12) = $102,482	($58,628 x 2) + ($932 x 42) + ($260 x 12) = $159,520
Off-Campus	($27,756 x 2) + ($476 x 42) + ($260 x 12) = $78,624	($34,071 x 2) + ($767 x 42) + ($260 x 12) = $103,476	($57,519 x 2) + ($932 x 42) + ($260 x 12) = $157,302
2-Year Graduation Dual Enrollment Savings Compared to 4-Year Graduation			
Average Savings	**$23,961**	**$25,686**	**$66,021**
Living with Family	$62,832 − $54,528 = $8,304	$95,540 − $83,104 = $12,436	$185,120 − $134,824 = $50,296
On-Campus	$108,584 − $77,404 = $31,180	$134,296 − $102,482 = $31,814	$234,512 − $159,520 = $74,992
Off-Campus	$111,024 − $78,624 = $32,400	$136,284 − $103,476 = $32,808	$230,076 − $157,302 = $72,774

The Ultimate Cost-Saving Strategy for a 2-year Graduation: What Marcus Did

To save as much as possible, you need to do the following: (1) earn college credits while in high school. If those credits are free or lower cost than assumed, you will save thousands of dollars more than estimated here, (2) take lots of classes during standard semesters and break periods, and (3) have a plan for the classes you will take and the order in which you will take them. This path is hard, but the rewards are massive.

Plan: A high school student dual enrolls at a community college. They take and pay for 18 credits during the summers of their junior and senior years of high school, for a total of 36 units. They will also take and pay for 12 more community college credits after starting college. They will do this by taking one 3-credit community college class per semester for four semesters. The student would only have to pay for 6 extra credit hours at their primary university.

Total Education Cost Formula: Total cost = 2 years in school + 48 lower-cost community college credits + 6 credits at their primary university not covered by tuition.

Figure 14			
Ultimate Cost-Saving 2-Year Graduation Dual Enrollment (What Marcus Did)			
Living Situation	**In-State Public**	**Private For-Profit**	**Private Nonprofit**
Living with Family	($15,708 x 2) + ($476 x 6) + ($260 x 48) = $46,752	($23,885 x 2) + ($767 x 6) + ($260 x 48) = $64,852	($46,280 x 2) + ($932 x 6) + ($260 x 48) = $110,632
On-Campus	($27,146 x 2) + ($476 x 6) + ($260 x 48) = $69,628	($33,574 x 2) + ($767 x 6) + ($260 x 48) = $84,230	($58,628 x 2) + ($932 x 6) + ($260 x 48) = $135,328
Off-Campus	($27,756 x 2) + ($476 x 6) + ($260 x 48) = 70,848	($34,071 x 2) + ($767 x 6) + ($260 x 48) = $85,224	($57,519 x 2) + ($932 x 6) + ($260 x 48) = $133,110
Ultimate Cost-Saving Plan Compared to 4-Year Graduation			
Average Savings	$31,737	$43,938	$90,213
Living with Family	$62,832 − $46,752 = $16,080	$95,540 − $64,852 = $30,688	$185,120 − $110,632 = $74,488
On-Campus	$108,584 − $69,628 = $38,956	$134,296 − $84,230 = $50,066	$234,512 − $135,328 = $99,184
Off-Campus	$111,024 − $70,848 = $40,176	$136,284 − $85,224 = $51,060	$230,076 − $133,110 = $96,966

Chapter 5 Workbook

1. Understanding the Costs of Different Types of Colleges

Given the average costs by school type, which is best for you: public, private, or not-for-profit?

_____

_____

_____

2. Cost of Delaying Graduation

Based on the colleges you are considering, how much extra would it cost if you take 5 years to graduate instead of 4? What are the other consequences of taking longer?

_____

_____

_____

3. Maximizing Credit Hours

If applicable, what will you do to get permission to take more credits than normal? What will you do to ensure you can handle the extra work?

_____

_____

_____

4. Dual Enrollment Benefits

How much money could you save by taking community college courses for your general education requirements?

_____

_____

_____

5. Creating a Cost-Saving Plan

After learning to save money and graduate early, what are the best strategies and plans for you? And why?

_____

_____

_____

Chapter 6: Finding the Right College for You

There's no such thing as the "perfect" school. Every college has strengths and weaknesses. So, don't seek "perfection." Instead, focus on what matters most to you and pick a school that aligns with your goals. Your school should help you graduate on time (or early), create a positive environment, and set you up for financial success. It is critical to pick the right school and major from day one. Students who choose a school that is not a good fit for them are more likely to end up unhappy, drop out, or waste time transferring to another school. These setbacks disrupt focus, drain enthusiasm, and often cost a lot of money. If you want to pick the right school the first time, pay close attention to this chapter.

How Much Should You Spend on College?

How much you spend on education should be based on your career goals and financial situation. The following section will help you decide how much to invest in your college education to get the best return.

High-Paying Careers: For the small percentage of people planning on entering high-paying, ultra-competitive fields, like law, hedge fund management, and private equity, a degree from a prestigious school can provide significant advantages. Top-tier schools can provide valuable connections and a strong reputation. Prestigious degrees can lead to great job prospects and millions more in lifetime earnings. If prestige and connections will help you land your high-paying dream job, investing more in your education is likely a smart choice. But, before you spend a fortune on a degree, make sure you are committed and have the skills to succeed doing hard, fast-paced, high-pressure, technically challenging work.

Standard Careers: An expensive degree is unnecessary for most jobs. If where you get the degree won't affect your opportunities or salary, choose the lowest-cost option. You can also earn all your general education credits at a local community college and then transfer to a higher-profile four-year in-state school.

In-State vs. Out-of-State Tuition: In-state public college tuition is usually much less expensive than tuition for out-of-state or private schools. Consider the financial advantages of attending an in-state school versus the higher-cost alternatives.

Do the Math for All Costs: College costs far more than just tuition. Research and plan for costs like housing, food, transportation, books, supplies, student loan interest, and hidden school fees. Living in an expensive city like New York will cost more than living in a cheaper area. So when you are comparing different colleges, consider all costs, not just tuition. Also, ensure your plan covers expenses that student loans may not cover. You can use the total cost calculator on our website to avoid getting caught off guard by unexpected costs and compare the cost of attending different colleges.

Graduate Early – Save Big

To graduate in half the time at half the cost, you must prioritize schools that allow you to transfer credits and graduate early. Every school has its own rules about what credits they accept and how many credits you can take. The more prestigious the school, the harder it typically is to transfer credits or graduate early. The more willing a school is to accept transfer credits and let you take extra classes, the more money and time you can save. If you have earned transfer credits, ensure the school(s) you are considering will accept them. Answer the following questions to create a plan to maximize your savings.

How many credits do I need to graduate? We assume you need 126; however, you may need more or less. The fewer you need, the faster you can usually graduate.

How many credits can I take per semester, and what is the overloading policy? Some public institutions, especially community colleges, charge by credit hour. A class is typically 3–4 credit hours; an elective may be the same or only 1–2 credit hours. To graduate in four years, you will need to complete 15–16 credits per semester, assuming your school requires 120–128 credits to graduate. Some schools also have a per-credit-hour price and a price for full-time students taking a minimum of 12 credits per semester. For example, when Marshall attended UT, the full-time price allowed students to take 12 to 18 credits per semester. Marshall took advantage of all 18 credits included in the full-time student price and then paid extra for taking more credits at UT and at a nearby community college. To save money, consider attending a school that has a reasonable cost per credit hour and, if applicable, allows full-time students to take a good number of credits (18+, for example) at no extra cost. The bottom line is that school will cost you less if you can take more credits at a lower price.

If you plan to exceed the standard amount of credit hours allowed per semester (for UT, it was 21 when Marshall attended), you must usually maintain a high GPA and meet other requirements to get approval. This is usually only applicable to students trying to graduate in under three years. Do your research and consider how many classes the colleges you are considering attending will allow you to take. Also, if you want to graduate fast, ask admissions about the appeals process and credit hour overloading policies. The bottom line is that the more classes you take/can take, the faster you can graduate.

How many credits will the school let me transfer? If you've earned transfer credits, make sure the school you are considering accepts all or most of them if you want to save money, graduate faster, and be rewarded for your hard work.

Can I take lower-cost community college courses while enrolled at a university? If a school accepts transfer credits from dual enrollment, you may be able to save hundreds of dollars per credit hour. If you are already taking the maximum number of credits covered by the price of full-time tuition, consider taking lower-cost community college courses at the same time. If you get approval and meet grade requirements, you will receive credit for them at the university you attend. You can also take lower-cost community college courses over the summer. Ask the colleges you are considering about their policies and where to find the list of community colleges and courses they will accept to meet your degree requirements.

What's the school's policy on College Level Examination Program (CLEP) exams? They are exams you can take to bypass general education requirements and/or get college credit. If a school accepts CLEP exams, you can, at best, save money and time by earning college credits at a low cost. Or, at a minimum, bypass introductory classes so you can focus on higher-level courses where you will learn far more valuable information.

Are the essential classes for my major offered year-round, or are they available only during specific times? Limited class availability can delay graduation and make early graduation very challenging. Ask colleges if they can guarantee they will have openings in the classes you need to graduate on time. Some classes are more important and have more limited availability than others, so schedule those first. Since electives are usually the least important, schedule them last. We cannot emphasize enough how important it is for you to sign up for classes as early as possible. If you don't sign up early, you may not get the classes you want or need.

Will the administration support my goal to graduate early? Make sure there are academic advisors who can make it easier for you to transfer any credits you have earned. Also, see if they can help you create a plan to graduate early. Ask if colleges support early graduation, how fast you could graduate, and how they can help you accomplish that goal. If a college doesn't want to help you with that goal, perhaps it is time to consider other schools.

What to Consider When Picking a College

You need a school that matches your needs and priorities. Consider academic rigor, location, extracurriculars, and other factors that are important to you. The key is to find schools that meet your needs and eliminate those that don't. This will help you narrow down your choices as much as possible.

Quality of Education: When it comes to education, it's all about what you value. Some schools focus on academic excellence to attract brilliant students. If you want to be part of a community of scholars, you'll want to choose a school known for its academic rigor. However, the athletic program may matter most if you're a serious athlete aiming for a sports career. Another consideration is that some schools force students to take certain classes. Marshall picked a school without a foreign language requirement because the subject was so challenging for him. The key is to choose a school that aligns with your abilities, goals, and ambitions.

Program Strengths: Not every school is strong in every subject. Some schools might be great for business. Others excel in engineering or the arts. Make sure the school you choose has a solid program for what you will be studying.

Graduation Rates: Graduation rates show how committed schools are to student success. A school with low graduation rates might not offer the support you need to succeed. High graduation rates usually mean better advising and more resources for students, which is a top indicator of the program's quality. Lower-cost schools with high acceptance rates usually have lower graduation rates, but the cost savings may be worth it for committed students.

Class Size and Support: Do you prefer small, intimate settings, or are large lecture halls fine? Some people need one-on-one attention, while others don't mind being a face in the crowd. Ensure the school's teaching format suits your individual needs. You may have to pay more for smaller class sizes, but it can be a good investment if that is what you need.

Graduating Early: Does the school accept AP, CLEP, and community college credits? What about dual enrollment courses? Can you fast-track your degree by taking more than the required number of courses? It's worth mentioning these things again because this book is all about helping you graduate faster and more economically.

Cost: What is the total cost for the school? Include fees per credit hour and semester, living expenses, travel, and anything else required. Is choosing a more expensive or economical school better depending on your future career requirements and pay?

Connections: It's not what you know but who you know. Does the school have strong alumni connections in your chosen field? Your career path matters. Connections can make or break your job prospects after graduation. If your field requires connections, choose a program that can help you. Otherwise, spend a lot of time networking.

Location, Weather, Opportunities, Amenities, Travel: Location matters a lot. Where you go to school can directly impact your well-being, happiness, and overall success. Some students want to stay close to home for the support of family and to keep housing costs low. Others are looking for a fresh start, maybe in a place with better weather or new opportunities. If sunshine keeps you motivated, or if you thrive in a place with four distinct seasons, don't ignore that. Your environment shapes your daily life. It can hurt your school performance if you don't like where you are. Also, consider the school's setting. Some universities are in the heart of bustling cities, while others are remote. City life can bring convenience and opportunities. Rural schools may be more peaceful but may lack amenities or job opportunities. Travel is often more expensive and time-consuming in a remote location or far from home.

Safety: Some top schools are in areas with high crime rates. It's worth checking the neighborhoods around your potential campus. If you can't visit in person, use Google Maps or online reviews to get a feel for it. Take Marcus, for example. He went to USC. It has great academics, but the surrounding neighborhood is unsafe. He had to weigh safety against the opportunities the school provided. That is a reality for many students in urban environments. So, consider location as a major factor when choosing a school.

Health: If you care about your health, prioritize your school's food options. Sure, more schools are offering healthier choices these days, but don't assume they all do. If a nutritious diet matters to you, research each school's dining services. See if they offer options that fit your needs. A healthy diet boosts your energy and mood. So, don't leave your food choices to chance. If the school you are considering does not have healthy options, consider meal prep services and/or getting groceries and cooking.

Political/Religious Beliefs: Many schools have a political bias. Research to see if your values align with the school's and if you are a good fit. Religion is another factor to think about. If faith plays a significant role in your life, you may prefer a school that reflects your values. If you are not religious, you may prefer a secular school. Either way, choosing a school that supports your beliefs and the community you are a part of is crucial. It may not be possible to find a school that shares your values. This can be a great test to evaluate and advocate for your beliefs.

School Culture: School culture is a huge factor in finding the right school for you. Each school has a unique vibe. Its academics, political and religious beliefs, diversity, clubs, sports, and Greek life shape it. Greek life can play a significant role. For some people, fraternities and sororities offer a strong sense of community. Schools where sports and parties rule can be a blast. But, if you want an education, those schools might not keep you on track. Just make sure you balance fun with academics. It's about finding a culture that will support your goals and make your college experience the best it can be, financially and socially.

Consider the Pros and Cons of Different Schools

Selecting the right college is about figuring out what matters most to you. For some, the school's prestige is most important. Others may value location, cost, or specific programs. Make a list of all the things you want in a college. Use the college selection criteria from this chapter for ideas. Also, include anything else that matters to you that we may not have mentioned. Rank those criteria by their importance in your college choice. Put the deal-breakers at the top. Use your list to narrow your choices of safety, target, and reach schools. Then, pick the best ones you will apply to.

Chapter 6 Workbook

1. How Much Should You Invest in an Education?

How much should you invest in college based on your future career earnings?

_____

_____

_____

_____

2. What Are Your Career Goals?

What kind of career do you envision for yourself? If applicable, how will your major and choice of college help you achieve your career goals?

_____

_____

_____

_____

_____

_____

3. Will the School(s) you're Considering Help You Graduate Early?

Research if the school(s) you are considering accept transfer credits, dual enrollment/credit, allow credit hour overloading, and offer the courses you need when you need them.

_____

_____

_____

_____

4. Based on Your Research, How Early Could You Reasonably Graduate, and What Would Be Your Plan?

_____

_____

_____

_____

_____

_____

5. What Do You Want and Need from a College?

Based on the "What to Consider When Picking a College" section of the book, list your top priorities when choosing a college (e.g., location, cost, academic rigor). List in order of highest priorities to lowest priorities.

1. _____   6. _____

2. _____   7. _____

3. _____   8. _____

4. _____   9. _____

5. _____   10. _____

Notes:_____

_____

_____

_____

_____

6. Academic Strengths

What are the academic strengths of the schools you're considering? Do those schools have reputable programs for your major?

_____

_____

_____

_____

_____

_____

_____

7. Connections and Alumni Network

How strong is the alumni network at the schools you're interested in? Could these connections help you in your future career?

_____

_____

_____

_____

8. Pros and Cons of Your Top Choices

Make a list of pros and cons for the top 3 schools you're considering. Use this list to evaluate which school is the best fit for you.

School #1

Pros	Cons
1. _____	1. _____
2. _____	2. _____
3. _____	3. _____
4. _____	4. _____
5. _____	5. _____

School #2

Pros	Cons
1. _____	1. _____
2. _____	2. _____
3. _____	3. _____
4. _____	4. _____
5. _____	5. _____

School #3

Pros	Cons
1. _____	1. _____
2. _____	2. _____
3. _____	3. _____
4. _____	4. _____
5. _____	5. _____

Notes:_____

_____

_____

_____

Chapter 7: Applying and Getting Into College

Everyone has their dream school, but not everyone gets accepted. Here's how to get into the best program you are qualified for.

Safety Schools: Schools you are almost sure to get into. Apply to a few schools where you are far more qualified than their average student. These schools should serve as your safety net.

Target Schools: Schools where you're about the same as their average student. These schools are your most realistic options and should be your top priority.

Reach Schools: These are the schools that are a big stretch—you might get in, but it's a long shot. If attending a prestigious school is a goal, you can always aim high, and if you do not get in, no harm, no foul.

Many students apply to 8–12 schools: Don't overdo it. Marshall only applied to the University of Tampa and Baylor and got into both. On the other hand, Marcus applied to ten schools: USC, UCLA, University of Pennsylvania, Cornell, NYU, UC Berkeley, UC San Diego, UC Irvine, UC Davis, and UC Santa Barbara. All accepted him.

The Secret to Great School Applications

The secret? Apply to fewer schools so you can create higher-quality applications with less stress. Research each school in depth. Then, create highly personalized applications. Your applications should show why you are an excellent fit for that school. We recommend applying to two to eight schools you have thoroughly considered, feel fully committed to, and have a strong chance of being accepted into. Never waste time or money applying to schools you're not serious about. Applying to fewer schools has the added benefit of saving time and mental energy so you can focus on academics, extracurriculars, possibly a part-time job, and enjoying your senior year of high school.

How Costs Add Up with College Applications

- College application fees range from $25 to $125+ (some are free).
- Applying to 6 colleges (2 safeties, 2 targets, 2 reaches) would cost around $300, assuming $50 per application.
- At $50 per application, applying to twelve colleges would cost about $600.
- Applying to 6 colleges instead of 12 would make the process much easier and likely save you several hundred dollars.

What Sets You Apart?

We once believed that getting into college was simply about good grades and solid SAT/ACT scores. But as we grew older, we realized that the game was more complex. It wasn't just about working hard; it was about working smart. The admissions process is much more than test scores and transcripts. It's about strategy. To get into your dream college, you must know the system, follow the rules, and, most importantly, stand out. Colleges are not just looking for anyone. They seek candidates who can add something unique to their community. You must show them you are the type of person they are looking for. So, as you brainstorm application ideas, ask yourself these questions.

What are my strengths? Identify where you shine academically and personally. Don't just think about the obvious; reflect on the best parts of you.

What am I passionate about? Passion is magnetic. Colleges want to see a spark in you that they can help grow into a powerful fire.

What unique experiences have shaped me? Maybe you've faced challenges that made you stronger or fostered personal growth. These stories matter, and you should make sure colleges know about them.

Building a Strong Academic Record

A lot of people assume that grades are the only thing that matters. They are important, but grades are just part of the equation. Colleges want to know if you can handle challenging classes. They want to see if you have challenged yourself in the past. This is the best proof you can give about being ready for future challenges. To do this, take the most challenging high school classes you can succeed in.

Take Advanced Placement (AP) or International Baccalaureate (IB) courses. Show colleges you can handle tough material.

Get help when you need it. The smartest thing you can do is to ask for help when you are struggling academically or emotionally. Yes, it might be a bit uncomfortable at first. But, if you want to reach your goals faster, get help from your peers, teachers, and counselors. It will make the process easier for you. After all, if you don't reach out, people won't know how to help or even that you need help in the first place.

Develop rock-solid study habits. Get work done as far in advance as possible and give your best effort. This will help you never miss assignments and perform at your highest level. You have just 24 hours in a day. So, use your time wisely to reach your goals, and don't forget to have some fun along the way.

The Power of Extracurricular Activities

If grades were everything, the admissions process would be simple. However, colleges want to build communities of well-rounded, multidimensional students, not just A-grade classrooms. They want students who are engaged in life, not just school. The question isn't just, "How smart are you?" It's, "What do you bring to the table?" This is where extracurriculars come into play.

Join clubs and organizations that reflect your passion: School teams or independent sports teach discipline and teamwork. Sports can help you develop and demonstrate your leadership skills. They can also help you grow by allowing you to face and overcome challenges.

Get involved in sports: Whether you're on a school team or do sports independently, athletics demonstrate discipline and teamwork. Sports can be another area where you show leadership and provide examples of obstacles you have overcome and the effort you have invested throughout high school.

Volunteer: Giving back to your community shows leadership and empathy. Colleges love students who contribute beyond themselves because those same students will often try to make whatever college they attend a better place.

Internships or part-time jobs: Get experience through internships or jobs, especially in fields related to your future career. You will gain valuable connections and skills that will help you prepare for college and adult life.

Why Leadership Matters

Don't just participate—lead. The difference between a leader and a follower can make or break your application. You must show that you're not afraid to take the reins to stand out. Colleges are looking for leaders who inspire others and do the hard work few are willing to do. Leadership is not about titles. It's about impact. Prove you have made a difference by showing colleges what you have done and why it matters.

Run for leadership positions: Colleges want to see you take on big responsibilities, and leading a club or a sports team can be a great way to stand out.

Organize events or projects: Don't wait for others to tell you what to do. Make things happen, whether it's organizing a fundraiser or starting a new club.

Launch your own initiative: Take your personal projects and passions to the next level. Building something from the ground up shows ambition. It takes courage to face new challenges, learn new things, and be yourself.

Demonstrating Interest

Colleges are more likely to admit students who show genuine interest in attending. To effectively demonstrate your interest, consider the following strategies:

Visit Campuses and Attend Open Houses or Information Sessions: If possible, visit the campus in person to get a feel for the environment. Attend open houses or scheduled information sessions to engage with staff and students.

Participate in Virtual Tours and Online Webinars: If you can't visit in person, show your interest by attending the college's virtual events.

Reach Out to Admissions Officers with Thoughtful Questions: Contact admissions officers with specific questions about academics (perhaps early graduation), campus life, or admissions. Thoughtful inquiries show your sincere interest.

Follow and Engage with the College's Social Media Accounts: Follow the college's social media accounts to stay updated on the latest events and news. Engage with posts and attend online events to demonstrate your interest further.

Knowing Why a College Is Right for You

Many applicants send generic applications to dozens of schools. They figure something will stick. But that's not how the game is played. Colleges want to know why you want to attend their school, and that's where the "Why Us" essay comes in.

Do your homework: Research what makes each college special. In your application, mention specific programs, professors, or opportunities that match your goals. You can also say if you like the location, have family nearby, or want to live and work near the college after graduation.

Show how you fit: Don't just say what the school offers. Explain why you would thrive there and how you'll contribute to the campus culture.

Mastering the Application Process

The college application process can be overwhelming. But if you break it down, it's manageable. Organization is key. Know your deadlines, keep your documents in order, and don't procrastinate. The following components need to come together for your application to be successful.

Completing College Applications: Many colleges accept the Common App or Coalition App, which allows you to apply to multiple schools using one platform. Some institutions require you to complete their applications instead of, or in addition to, the Common or Coalition Application.

Personal Statement: This is your chance to tell your unique story. Be authentic and reflective. Share experiences that shaped you and your goals. Let your personality and voice come through.

Supplemental Essays: Tailor each essay to the specific college and prompt. Show your knowledge of and enthusiasm for the school. Explain why you're a good fit and how the college aligns with your goals.

Resume: Highlight your academic achievements, extracurricular involvement, leadership roles, work experience, and any special projects or accomplishments. Provide a well-rounded view of your activities and contributions beyond the classroom.

Standardized Test Scores: Although many colleges have adopted test-optional policies, submitting strong SAT or ACT scores can still enhance your application, especially if they align with the school's expectations.

Letters of Recommendation (LOR)

Choosing Recommenders: Choosing the right recommenders is crucial. Their letters of recommendation will reveal your strengths, character, and achievements. Choose recommenders who know you well. They should write meaningful, personalized letters. This will strengthen your application and provide a more complete picture of you. Here's who you should consider asking for a letter of recommendation:

Teachers in Core Academic Subjects: Choose teachers who have taught you in subjects like English, math, science, or history. Ideally, these high school teachers have seen you grow as a student. They should also be able to talk about your academic performance, work ethic, curiosity, and pursuits. Consider finding teachers whose classes relate to what you will study in college. This will give a college even more confidence that you are passionate about the subject.

Counselors: Some school counselors can provide a broader view of your high school career, including your academic achievements, personal growth, extracurricular activities, and contributions to the school.

Coaches, Employers, or Mentors: They can offer additional perspectives on your leadership, teamwork, and initiative outside the classroom, as well as speak to your character and how you've demonstrated responsibility in various settings.

Requesting Letters of Recommendation

When requesting letters of recommendation, it's important to approach your recommenders thoughtfully and with plenty of preparation. You'll help your recommenders write strong, personalized letters that enhance your application by giving them the time and information they need. Here's how to ask for a LOR:

Ask Early: Contact your recommenders more than a month before the deadline. This gives them plenty of time to write a detailed, thoughtful letter.

Provide a Resume or List of Achievements: Help your recommenders by providing them with a resume or a list of your accomplishments, activities, and awards. This will give them concrete details to highlight in their letter.

Share College and Application Details: Let your recommenders know which colleges you're applying to and anything specific you'd like them to address. For example, if a college values leadership or community involvement, mention this so they can tailor their letter accordingly.

Following Up With Recommenders

Once your recommenders have agreed to write your letters of recommendation, it's important to communicate and show appreciation. By maintaining good communication and expressing gratitude, you build solid and lasting relationships with your recommenders, who have played a key role in your college journey. Here's how to stay organized and courteous:

Send Gentle Reminders: Ask your recommenders to give you a date when the LOR will be completed. Politely remind them of the upcoming submission deadlines as they approach. This will help them stay on track without feeling rushed.

Thank Them for Their Time and Effort: A sincere thank-you note and gift show appreciation for the time and thought they have put into your letter. Little gestures like a handwritten note or a heartfelt email can make a positive, lasting impression.

Keep Them Updated: Once you receive college admissions decisions, update your recommenders on your progress. Let them know where you have been accepted and your final decision. They will appreciate knowing how their support helped.

Beyond the Basics: Thinking Outside the Box

A positive online presence will boost your application in today's digital age. It will give admissions officers a better sense of your interests and professionalism.

Create a LinkedIn Profile: Highlight your academics, extracurriculars, volunteer work, and any internships or jobs you have completed or are currently doing. This professional platform allows you to connect with others in your field of interest and present a polished version of yourself to colleges.

Start a Blog or YouTube Channel: If you're passionate about a topic, share your knowledge in a blog or on YouTube.

Make Sure Your Social Media Reflects the Best Version of You: Check your profiles. They should match the image you want to project. Colleges may check applicants' online profiles. Ensure your content is respectful and shows your values and achievements.

Staying Organized and Managing Stress

College applications can sometimes be overwhelming. But, if you stay organized, it will be easier. Here are some strategies to help you stay on top of everything.

Create a Detailed Application Calendar: List all deadlines for applications, essays, financial aid, and scholarships. Break tasks into smaller steps, such as requesting letters of recommendation or submitting transcripts, and assign deadlines for each step.

Use Tools to Track Your Progress: Spreadsheets or apps like Trello, Google Sheets, or Notion can help you organize tasks and track progress. You can create sections for each school and monitor what has been completed and what is left to do.

Take Regular Breaks and Practice Self-Care: To avoid burnout, schedule regular breaks. Practice self-care by getting enough sleep, exercising, and engaging in activities that help reduce stress, such as spending time with friends and family.

Application Timeline	
1. Junior Year **Begin researching colleges** to understand which are a good fit. **Take standardized tests** (SAT, ACT) and consider retaking them if necessary. **Build your resume** by engaging in extracurricular activities, leadership roles, and possibly community service.	**2. Summer Before Senior Year** **Start your personal statement** and supplemental essays. Starting early gives you more time to write with less pressure. **Begin working on your college applications** and gathering your transcripts and test scores.
3. Fall of Senior Year **Finalize and submit your college applications**. Pay close attention to early decision or early action deadlines. **Request letters of recommendation** from teachers, counselors, and mentors.	**4. Winter of Senior Year** **Follow up** on submitted applications to ensure they're complete. **Continue applying for scholarships** as long as deadlines are still open.
5. Spring of Senior Year **Review your college acceptances** and financial aid offers. **Make your decision:** Notify the school you will attend by the deadline.	

Chapter 7 Workbook

1. Safety, Target, and Reach Schools

List the schools you're considering as "safety," "target," and "reach" schools. Why did you categorize each school this way?

1. Safety_____   2. Safety_____

3. Target_____   4. Target_____

5. Reach_____   6. Reach_____

2. Your Strengths

What are your top academic and personal strengths? How do these strengths make you a valuable student to colleges?

_____

_____

_____

3. Passions

What are you most passionate about? Using your application, how can you show off that passion to colleges?

_____

_____

_____

4. Unique Experiences

What unique experiences have you had or could you have to help your application stand out in a good way?

_____

_____

_____

5. Building a Strong Academic Record

What will you do to strengthen your academic record and have a better application?

_____

_____

_____

6. Extracurricular Commitments

What clubs, sports, or organizations are you involved in? How have you shown dedication to these activities? How will you mention them in your college application?

_____

_____

_____

7. Leadership Roles

Have you taken on leadership positions in any of your extracurricular activities? If yes, how have you demonstrated leadership? If you have not yet taken on any leadership roles, how could you do so moving forward?

_____

_____

_____

_____

8. Why Are You Interested in This College?

Pick one college you're applying to and research what makes it special. Why do you want to attend, and how would you contribute to the campus community?

_____

_____

_____

9. Demonstrating Interest

How will you demonstrate your interest in one or more colleges to help support your application?

_____

_____

_____

10. The Right Fit for You

How will you show you are a good fit for the college you are applying to?

_____

_____

_____

11. Your Personal Statement

What story will you tell in your personal statement? How does this story reflect your personality, values, and aspirations?

_____

_____

_____

12. Resume and Achievements

Outline your academic achievements, extracurricular involvement, leadership roles, and work experience. How do these experiences highlight your strengths and contributions?

_____

_____

_____

13. Choosing Recommenders

Who are the best people to write your letters of recommendation, and why? How well do they know your strengths and character?

_____

_____

_____

14. Your Online Presence

How will you use your online presence to show schools and employers why they should want you on their team?

_____

_____

_____

15. Managing Stress

What positive strategies will you use to manage stress during the application process? How do you balance self-care with your responsibilities?

_____

_____

_____

Chapter 8: Paying for Your Education

This chapter is your guide to navigating the confusing world of paying for college. Many students and families underestimate the true cost of college, which goes far beyond tuition. Because college is so expensive, let's look at some great ways to pay for it.

Understanding the True Cost of College

Remember, tuition is just the tip of the iceberg when budgeting for college. Schools may provide cost estimates for expenses, but these figures are averages. Researching all possible expenses gives you a better idea of what you'll need to pay for. In addition to the cost of taking classes, the total cost of college includes the following:

Room and Board: Many schools offer several housing options at different price points. Find the best option for you quickly because housing can fill up fast. Then, based on your needs, find the best meal plan and incorporate it into your budget. For instance, if you eat three meals a day, you would need 3 x 7 = 21 meals in your weekly meal plan. Some students do 2 x 7 = 14 meals on their weekly plan and eat a cheaper breakfast in their dorm room.

Books and Supplies: Computer, textbooks, and other necessary academic supplies.

Transportation: The cost of using a service like Uber, local bus lines, or whatever is applicable to you. If you own a car, consider the costs for insurance, gas, repairs and maintenance, and parking fees.

Personal Expenses: These are the daily essential items you need that were not previously mentioned.

Loans May Not Cover Everything: Student loans can be helpful. But, they may not cover all expenses. This is especially true if you take extra courses or enroll in summer classes. Loans have borrowing limits; if you choose to attend an expensive school, you may need more money. Having a backup plan for covering additional costs is essential. Consider scholarships, part-time work, family support, and additional loan options.

Keep Your Family Informed and Involved: Financial transparency with your family is critical. Discussing college costs early allows everyone to plan and set realistic expectations. Understanding the financial support your family can or cannot provide will prevent last-minute stress and help you create a better financial plan before enrolling.

Understanding Student Loans

Student loans are a common way to fund college, but knowing the different loan options and their impact on your financial future is essential. We want you to be strong financially, so we will tell you how to get out of debt before discussing how to get into it.

1. **Plan for Repayment:** Before you borrow, know your repayment responsibilities and plan to repay your loans! Federal loans have more repayment flexibility than private loans, so they should be a first choice.

2. **Limit Borrowing:** Only borrow what you need to cover educational expenses. Avoid unnecessary loans. More debt now means much more to repay in the future.

3. **Understanding the Terms:** Read and compare the terms of every loan. Focus on interest rates, repayment options, and deferment opportunities to find the best terms. Exercise additional caution with private loans, as the terms can be harsher.

4. **Start with Federal Loans:** Always choose federal loans first if you need funds. They have lower rates and flexible repayment options.

Repayment Strategies for Student Loans

1. **Pay Off Your Loans as Fast as Possible:** The faster you pay off your student loans, the less interest you'll pay. This is why we recommend graduating early and paying down student loans as soon as you can.

2. **Pay High-Interest Loans First:** Loans with higher interest rates cost you more over time than loans with low interest rates. Paying off higher interest rate loans first will reduce the total amount you need to repay, saving you lots of money. After the high-interest-rate loans are paid off, start paying against the lower-interest-rate loans. While paying off the higher interest rate loans, make only the minimum payments on any lower interest rate loans you have.

3. **Standard Repayment Plan:** The standard repayment plan requires fixed monthly payments for ten years. Monthly payments may be higher than those for longer repayment plans, but you'll be debt-free sooner and pay less overall.

4. **Income-Driven Repayment Plans (IDR):** These plans set your payments based on your income and family size. They are more manageable if you have a low salary after graduation because IDR plans lower your monthly payment. After twenty to twenty-five years, any unpaid balance may be forgiven. Monthly payments are smaller. But, you'll pay more in total over time due to the longer repayment period. At the time of writing, some IDR plans have been stopped, at least temporarily, by the government, so check for up-to-date information if you are considering an IDR plan.

Types of Income-Driven Repayment (IDR) Plans

These plans help you manage your student loan payments. They base your payments on your income, not your debt. Consider these options if you qualify for an IDR plan.

Income-Based Repayment (IBR): IBR caps your payment at a percentage of your discretionary income. It's a great option if your income is low compared to your debt. But this plan extends your loan term, so you will have to pay for a longer time.

Pay as You Earn (PAYE): PAYE is another smart option, especially if you're early in your career and not making much money yet. PAYE also limits your payments to a percentage of your income and offers a forgiveness option after 20 years.

Revised Pay as You Earn (REPAYE): Like PAYE, but everyone qualifies. Plus, the government will help cover some of the interest, which keeps your debt from growing out of control. But it lacks the cap that PAYE has, so if your income rises, so will your monthly payments.

Income-Contingent Repayment (ICR): This one is a bit more flexible. It lets you pay based on your income and has fewer eligibility restrictions. It's not as generous as the others in capping your payment. But it could be an option if you don't qualify for the other plans.

Public Service Loan Forgiveness (PSLF)

PSLF forgives your loans after 120 qualifying payments (ten years). You must work full-time for a qualifying public service employer, such as a government agency or a nonprofit.

- **Eligibility:** You must be enrolled in an income-driven repayment plan to qualify.
- **Benefits:** Your loan balance is forgiven after 10 years of qualifying payments. This can greatly reduce your total repayment.
- **Consideration:** Your job and repayment plan must meet the program's requirements to qualify for forgiveness. Missing or late payments can also disqualify you.

Federal Loans (Best Option)

The US government funds federal student loans. They have lower interest rates and more flexible repayment options than private loans and should be your first option when borrowing for college.

Subsidized Federal Loans (1st Choice)

- **Eligibility:** For undergraduate students with demonstrated financial need.
- **Interest:** These loans are called subsidized loans because the government saves you a lot of money by covering interest costs while you're in school, 6 months after leaving, and during deferment.
- **Benefit:** This is the most affordable loan option because of temporary interest deferment.

Unsubsidized Federal Loans (2nd Choice)

- **Eligibility:** Available to both undergraduate and graduate students, regardless of financial need.

- **Interest:** With unsubsidized loans, you are charged interest from the day you receive the loan until it is paid off. The longer you take to pay these loans back, the more they will cost you.

- **Benefit:** Although interest accrues immediately, unsubsidized loans provide essential funding for students who need additional financial support. The interest rates are higher than those of subsidized loans but lower than those of parent PLUS loans.

Parent PLUS Loans (3rd Choice)

Parent PLUS loans are federal loans that parents can take out to help cover the cost of their child's education. These loans fill the gaps that other loans don't cover. Because they have higher interest rates and make a parent responsible for the student's debts, they should be a last resort for government loan types.

- **Eligibility:** Parents of dependent undergraduates can apply for these loans. They can borrow up to the total cost of attendance minus other financial aid.

- **Interest:** These loans have fixed rates. They are usually higher than those for subsidized or unsubsidized loans. The interest also accumulates while you're in school.

- **Repayment:** This starts after the loan is fully disbursed. Deferment options are available.

Private Loans (Last Choice)

Private loans come from various financial institutions. They usually have higher interest rates and accumulate interest while you are in school. They have fewer and less flexible repayment options than federal loans. For these reasons, they are a last resort.

- **Interest Rates:** Often based on your credit score or your cosigner's credit score. There are fixed and variable rate options.

- **Repayment Terms:** Private loans usually have stricter terms. They offer limited deferment options and less repayment flexibility.

- **When to Consider:** Only pursue private loans after exhausting all federal loan options because they are generally more expensive and less lenient.

FAFSA: The First Step in Your Financial Aid Journey

Asking for financial help starts with a form that too many people overlook: FAFSA. Filing the Free Application for Federal Student Aid (FAFSA) is not just a step in the process—it is *the* step. It's your entry ticket, your gateway to tapping into financial aid from the government. You might be thinking, "Why bother? It's just another form, right?" But it's much more than that. FAFSA is your key to federal grants, work-study programs, and student loans. The bottom line is that if you don't file for the FAFSA each year, the government and many schools cannot provide you with financial aid.

The Key to Unlocking Financial Aid

FAFSA doesn't just randomly give out cash. It uses a formula based on you and your family's finances to tell the government what aid you qualify for. Now, let's break down the types of aid that FAFSA can unlock for you.

Federal Work-Study Program: Learn and Earn

Work-study is a need-based program, so it is only available to students who demonstrate financial need. Work-study jobs let you earn money for school while also building your work ethic and experience. The best part is that these positions are designed to accommodate students' needs.

Part-Time Employment: Opportunities Beyond Work-Study

On-Campus Jobs: Whether you are in the work-study program or not, you can usually find part-time jobs on campus. Jobs in gyms, dining halls, libraries, student centers, or administrative offices are often available to all students. These positions typically offer flexible hours to help you balance work and academics. You can also work with the school or independently to tutor your peers. Marshall and Marcus worked as independent tutors to make extra money in college.

Off-Campus Jobs: Another option is working for a local business. Many students find part-time jobs in retail, restaurants, or even internships related to their field of study. Employers near colleges often hire students and offer flexible hours.

Supplement Your Income: Working part-time, whether on or off-campus, can provide you with the income you need to cover personal expenses like books, supplies, or entertainment. Earning money can also reduce your reliance on student loans, helping you avoid accumulating unnecessary debt.

Gaining Workforce Experience: Employers prefer hiring people with a strong work history because, most likely, those same people will keep working hard. Before hiring you, employers may require a recommendation from your past employer. So, work hard and be respectful of all your bosses so you can get a recommendation when you need it. Even if a job isn't your favorite, it can be a big step toward your dream career.

Employer Tuition Assistance

Many companies offer tuition assistance or reimbursement programs to help their employees pursue further education. These programs are a great way to advance your career while getting help with college costs.

What It Covers: Employer tuition assistance programs may help pay for classes, certifications, tutoring, supplies, and degree programs relevant to your job.

Conditions to Consider: Most tuition assistance programs have conditions. These include a minimum GPA requirement, finishing your degree on schedule, and staying with the company for a time after you graduate. Some employers may require that your degree relate to your job or career path within the company.

How to Access Employer Tuition Assistance

Talk to HR: Your company's HR department can tell you about tuition assistance programs. Some companies may cover anything school-related. Others have annual limits or specific things they cover.

Plan Strategically: If your employer offers tuition assistance, consider how you can maximize this benefit. For example, you might work part-time for a company while in school or work full-time and go to school part-time to get tuition assistance.

Key Tip: Many large companies, such as Chipotle, Starbucks, and Walmart, offer generous tuition assistance programs to their employees. Check with your employer to see if any are available.

Balancing Work and Studies

Working part-time can help you manage your college expenses, but it's important to remember that your main job in college is to be a good student. Working as much as possible to earn more money may be tempting. However, too much work can hurt your academic performance. Most experts recommend working no more than ten to fifteen hours per week if you're a full-time student.[15] Figure out what is right for you. Make sure you have some time for fun, and don't spread yourself too thin. Your schedule will fill up quickly between classes, homework, and work shifts, so keep track of your commitments and avoid overloading yourself.

---

[15] Kerr, E., & Cabral, A. R. (n.d.). *"Weighing the pros and cons of working while in college."* US News.

State and Institutional Aid – Extra Money You Don't Want to Miss

You've heard us talk about FAFSA, but here's what most people miss: It's not just about federal aid. Filing FAFSA opens the door to state and college-specific aid, too.

State Aid: Don't Forget About Your Home Turf

Many states have their own financial aid programs for students who live and attend college within the state. These programs can offer generous grants and scholarships that can reduce your out-of-pocket costs. Many of these programs are *first-come, first-served*. The sooner you apply, the better your chances of securing those funds. Remember, you likely won't get funding if you don't fill out FAFSA.

Grants and Scholarships: States like to invest in their own, so many states have financial aid programs for residents attending in-state schools. Research your state's higher education agency to determine available programs and how to apply.

Other State Assistance Programs: States don't stop at grants and scholarships. Many also offer work-study programs and state-specific loans with favorable terms.

Institutional Aid: Colleges Want to Help You, Too

Now, let's talk about another big player—*your school*. You might not realize it, but colleges and universities have financial aid programs that can be just as valuable or more valuable than federal or state aid. Schools want to attract and support students, and one way they do that is by offering need and merit-based scholarships and grants. Here's the kicker: Many schools rely on your FAFSA to determine how much aid you qualify for. FAFSA doesn't just tell the government about your financial situation—it also tells your school, so fill it out!

College-Specific Scholarships and Grants: Every school is different. But, most have a fund to help students with tuition, fees, and housing.

Need-Based and Merit-Based Aid: Institutional aid typically falls into two categories: need-based and merit-based. Need-based aid is awarded based on your FAFSA. It shows the school how much help you need financially. Merit-based aid looks at your academic achievements, talents, or extracurricular activities. Merit-based scholarships may not rely on your FAFSA, but schools often use it to make decisions.

Grants – Unlocking Free Money for College

Grants are one of the most valuable types of financial aid you can receive. Why? Because grants are essentially free money that does not need to be repaid. Unlike loans, grants are awarded based on financial need and are meant to help students from various economic backgrounds access education. We have already covered state and institutional grants in the previous paragraphs. Now, let's explore federal and private grants. We'll also discuss the best strategies to maximize your chances of getting them.

Federal Grants

Federal grants are primarily need-based, and the amount you receive depends on your family's economic situation. Once again this is determined by the FAFSA.

Pell Grant: This federal grant is awarded to undergraduate students with significant financial need. The amount varies yearly but can be sizable and help cover a wide range of expenses, including tuition, fees, housing, and books.

Federal Supplemental Educational Opportunity Grant (FSEOG): This grant is for students with exceptional financial need. It is often awarded in addition to the Pell Grant. Unlike the Pell Grant, FSEOG funds are limited, so not every qualified student will receive the grant. FSEOG is awarded on a first-come, first-served basis, so applying early is crucial.

TEACH Grant: This targets students who plan to become teachers in high-need fields. There's a catch. If you don't teach after graduation, the grant becomes a loan that must be repaid. So, make sure you're committed to the path before applying.

Private Grants – Free Money from Outside Sources

Organizations, foundations, and corporations also offer grants to support students' education. These grants often have specific eligibility criteria, such as the field of study, demographic background, or career goals.

Where to Look: Professional associations, community organizations, and foundations offer grants to students pursuing specific career paths, such as STEM, education, or public service. Explore opportunities that align with your academic or career aspirations.

Additional Alternative Funding Options

Crowdfunding: Promoting your campaign is hard work. But it can be a creative way to seek help from friends, family, and even strangers who support your educational goals.

Apprenticeships and Trade Programs: Many apprenticeship and trade programs offer paid training if you're considering a career in a skilled trade or technical field. These programs often lead to solid jobs without needing a four-year degree.

The Game Plan: Maximizing Your Aid

1. **Gather Necessary Documents:** Before starting your FAFSA, have everything ready. This includes tax returns, W-2s, bank statements, and details of any untaxed income. Use the IRS Data Retrieval Tool. It will save you time and reduce errors by importing your tax info directly from the IRS into your FAFSA. Preparation will save you time, ensure accuracy, and improve results.

2. **Double-Check for Accuracy:** Accuracy is essential. Use official documents, like tax returns and W-2s, to ensure your financial data is accurate. Even a small error can delay your application and reduce your chances of receiving aid.

3. **Seek Advice If Needed:** Don't hesitate to ask for help. Your school's financial aid office and the FAFSA website offer resources to guide you.

4. **Submit Early:** The first rule of financial aid is to submit your FAFSA as soon as it opens on October 1. Many organizations award grants and scholarships on a first-come, first-served basis. The earlier you submit, the more likely you are to receive aid before funds run out.

5. **Understand the Verification Process:** If the system selects your FAFSA for verification, don't panic. It's a standard process. You will need to provide extra documents, like tax returns or income statements. Be prompt in gathering these materials to avoid delays.

6. **Review Your Student Aid Report (SAR):** After submitting your FAFSA, you'll receive a Student Aid Report (SAR). Review it in detail to identify any errors or inconsistencies. If you need to make corrections, submit them without delay so your aid can be correctly processed.

7. **Explore Additional Aid:** Beyond FAFSA, apply for other financial aid. There's a lot of money out there. The next chapter will discuss private scholarships. Also, check for state grants and college-specific scholarships. Determine their deadlines and requirements. Once again, FAFSA is usually used to determine eligibility.

8. **Renew Annually:** FAFSA isn't a one-time application; you must renew it yearly. Set reminders and ensure you complete it on time to maintain your eligibility for aid.

Chapter 8 Workbook

1. Beyond Tuition: Estimating College Costs

List all potential costs you might face during college beyond just tuition (e.g., housing, books, transportation). How will you plan and budget for these expenses?

_____

_____

2. Discussing Finances with Family

Have you discussed college costs with your family? What contributions can they make, and if possible, how will you work together to cover expenses?

_____

_____

3. Federal vs. Private Loans

Why are federal loans usually a better option than private loans?

_____

_____

4. Borrowing Responsibly

What steps can you take to ensure you can repay any student loans after college? What will your repayment strategy be?

_____

_____

5. Working Part-Time While in School

How could working while in college help you gain valuable skills and help you cover some of your costs? How will you balance work and academics?

_____

_____

6. Federal/State/Institutional/Private Aid and Grants

Research what aid/grant opportunities you are eligible for and how to apply for them.

_____

_____

Chapter 9: Winning Scholarships

Everyone loves free money, and that's exactly what scholarships are—money you don't have to pay back. Think of scholarships as strategic tools to get ahead. They come from various sources—colleges, private organizations, and nonprofits. Scholarships can be based on merit, need, leadership, talents, or other qualifications. They are not just for valedictorians or star athletes. If you're strategic, you may find great scholarships to help you pay for college so you won't have to take on as much debt. But here's the catch: Scholarships won't just fall into your lap. You've got to work hard applying for them. Take Marcus, for example. He won multiple scholarships that covered all his tuition and living expenses while attending USC. That didn't happen by luck—it took a lot of work. Scholarships changed Marcus's life, and they can help you, too.

Helping Others Win – Real Results, Real Impact

Marcus helped himself and other students win a combined total of over $500,000 in scholarships from big names like Google, Wells Fargo, Boeing, Volkswagen, PG&E, and Lockheed Martin. These students were not always the top of their class or star athletes. Many were regular students who worked hard and followed a strategy. Today, many have graduated and are in far less debt as a result of the scholarships they have won. Just imagine how amazing it would feel at your college graduation ceremony, diploma in hand, knowing you have far less debt because you earned scholarships.

"Marcus helped me use many of the strategies in this book to win scholarships, which helped me pay for my education at Rice University. The scholarships played a key role in my success, both academically and professionally, ultimately helping me land my dream position at NASA."
–Dante G.

Dante's story is a testament to the power of hard work, strategy, and early planning. In high school, he excelled as valedictorian while leading the robotics team and the business club, setting the stage for a bright future. By using the scholarship-winning strategies outlined by Marcus, Dante secured thousands of dollars in scholarships, which paved the way for his success at Rice University. There, he graduated magna cum laude in mechanical engineering while leading the Rice Eclipse Rocketry Team. Today, as a space flight controller at NASA, Dante's journey proves that with determination, careful planning, and the right resources, it's possible to achieve extraordinary goals while minimizing the financial burden of higher education.

Types of Scholarships

Merit-based scholarships: These scholarships recognize students for their exceptional performance in specific areas like academics or athletics.

Need-based scholarships: These scholarships are awarded based on financial need. They help students from low-to middle-income families afford college.

Community service scholarships: For students with exceptional volunteer work or community involvement.

Field-specific scholarships: These are designed for students pursuing specific fields of study, such as engineering, health care, etc. These scholarships often come from organizations or companies that seek to support students in specific industries.

Where to Find Scholarships

1. **Check with Your High School Guidance Counselor for Local Scholarships:** Many local organizations offer scholarships for students in your area or at your school. Your counselor can guide you to these opportunities. They are often less competitive because there are fewer total applicants.

2. **Explore Opportunities Through Community Organizations, Religious Institutions, and Employers:** Local clubs, religious groups, and employers may offer scholarships. Check if your parents' or family's employers offer scholarships. These scholarships also have fewer applicants, so they offer better odds of winning.

3. **Research Scholarships Offered by the College(s) You Are Applying to:** Many colleges provide merit-based or need-based scholarships to admitted students. Check each school's financial aid website for details and application requirements.

4. **Utilize Scholarship Search Engines and Databases:** Sites like Fastweb and Scholarship.com let you filter scholarships by your strengths. This makes it easier to find the right fit. The College Board Scholarship Search can also help you find scholarships that match your skills and interests.

Crafting Strong Scholarship Applications

1. Commence Your Search Early – Time Is an Advantage:

The earlier you start looking for scholarships, the more opportunities you'll have. Many scholarships have early deadlines. Waiting until the last minute limits your options. Starting early gives you time to apply for more scholarships. It also shows committees that you're dedicated, organized, and serious. Earlier applications have higher success rates. Committees notice students who show enthusiasm and initiative. By starting early, you also avoid stress and the last-minute rush that can lead to mistakes or weaker applications. Early applicants have more time to craft thoughtful essays, gather strong recommendations, and fine-tune their applications. The best time to apply for scholarships is in the fall when students are focused on college applications and there is less competition.

2. Diversify Your Applications – Cast a Wide Net:

Scholarships come in many forms: local, state, national, and international. Each offers unique opportunities. Local scholarships or those with unique criteria have fewer applicants, so you have a better chance of winning. National and international scholarships may offer bigger awards with more competition.

3. Strategize Your Applications – Work Smarter, Not Harder:

Applying for scholarships is not a numbers game; it's about being strategic. Prioritize scholarships with good-sized rewards where your qualifications give you a competitive edge. Some scholarships are easier to win because they are for your specific academic, athletic, or community background. Plan ahead by developing a scholarship application timeline and submitting applications a week before the deadline. This gives you time for last-minute revisions or unexpected events.

4. Attention to Detail – Make Every Application Count

Write Clear, Concise, and Persuasive Essays: Focus on creating well-structured essays that tell your story authentically. Connect your experiences and goals to the values or mission of the scholarship. In the scholarship game, details matter. Even a small mistake can hurt your chances. So make every application your best work.

Follow Instructions Precisely: Adhere to each scholarship's specific eligibility criteria and application instructions. Make sure you meet all the requirements, from GPA to extracurricular activities. Follow instructions closely. Submit exactly what the instructions request—including word count and formatting. Ensure you meet all deadlines, provide the necessary documents, and follow the guidelines to avoid wasting time by being disqualified.

Submit Flawless Applications: Check everything multiple times—essays, forms, and other documents. An error-free, well-written application shows your professionalism and attention to detail. It will boost your credibility with the selection committee.

5. Secure Recommendations Promptly – Get Strong Support

A strong recommendation letter can make or break your application. Ask for recommendations early. Give your teachers, mentors, or employers time to craft thoughtful, personalized letters. Tell them about the scholarship. Also, say what you hope they can emphasize in their letter. It's smart to gather more letters than you need. Some scholarships require specific recommendations (academic, personal, or professional). So it's good to have a few on hand for flexibility. Keep digital copies ready in a PDF format for easy submission. Also, ask your recommenders for permission to change the "To [name/scholarship committee]" part of the letter so you can personalize it for every scholarship committee without them having to resend it. Personalization will help you win!

6. Aligning with Organizational Values – Show Them Why You're a Fit

Scholarship providers want to invest in students who align with their missions and values. When applying for scholarships, it's essential to show how your goals, values, and achievements connect with the organization's objectives.

Highlight Your Achievements and Experiences in a Compelling Way: Showcase your academic, extracurricular, and personal accomplishments. Frame your experiences to emphasize leadership, initiative, and impact on others. Reflect on your values and how they connect to the scholarship's purpose. If you're applying for a leadership or community service scholarship, highlight your relevant experiences. Position yourself as someone who can carry on the organization's legacy.

Why It's Important: Scholarship committees want to invest in students who will represent their values and carry their mission forward. Demonstrating how your personal and professional goals align with the scholarship provider's vision makes you stand out from the crowd.

Powerful Approaches for Winning Scholarships

In the competitive world of scholarships, creating a standout application isn't just about meeting the requirements—it's about setting yourself apart from the competition. While many applicants will have strong grades, extracurriculars, and essays, those who go the extra mile with creativity, originality, and strategic presentation will rise above the rest. You need to think outside the box. That means using one or more of the innovative approaches outlined below to showcase your strengths, experiences, and unique qualities. Doing this will help you capture the attention of scholarship committees and increase your chances of success.

1. Personalize Your Essays – Make It Personal, Make It Powerful

Your essay is your voice. It's where you can show who you are beyond your resume and grades. Your essays must be personal and authentic. They should reflect your unique journey to stand out. Personal stories provide context to your accomplishments and give the committee a sense of how you will achieve your goals in the future. Share experiences that have shaped your character, values, and aspirations. Avoid clichés and overused responses. Instead, dig deep into your life story and share valuable insights and lessons. Write with passion and authenticity. Connect with readers by being vulnerable, showing growth, and having ambition in the areas they respect.

2. Showcase Multidisciplinary Skills – Be More Than One-Dimensional

In today's fast-paced world, scholarship committees want students who can excel in many areas. Showing that you're adaptable and capable of connecting ideas across different disciplines sets you apart. It signals versatility and innovation—traits that committees love. Make sure to highlight how you've combined knowledge from various subjects to solve problems or create projects. For instance, making A+B=C.

3. Create a Comprehensive Portfolio – Show, Don't Just Tell

Many students mention the awards they earned when applying for scholarships, but only a small number create a portfolio that visually represents their achievements. A portfolio brings your journey to life. It demonstrates your commitment, creativity, and the depth of your experiences. Include a diverse collection of your work. This can be art, research papers, achievements, or personal projects. Even if not directly asked for, a digital portfolio starting with your biggest accomplishments gives the committee a tangible sense of your capabilities and dedication.

4. Engage in Community Service – Show You're Committed to Impact

Committees are often looking for students who want to make a difference. Consistent involvement in community service demonstrates your dedication to helping others. Community service also showcases your empathy and commitment to social change—qualities that align with the values of many scholarship providers. Highlight long-term, meaningful community service projects where you've made an impact. Explain what you did, why you did it, and what you learned from the experience.

5. Leverage Social Media – Make Your Online Presence Work for You

Like it or not, scholarship committees may check your online presence. Use social media as a tool to showcase your projects, passions, and the positive impact you are making. A strong online presence can boost your application. It shows committees your personality, interests, and commitment. Clean up your profiles and make sure your online presence matches how you want to be viewed by others.

6. Establish a Profit or Nonprofit Organization – Show Initiative

Starting your own business or nonprofit is a bold move. It demonstrates that you're not just a student but a change-maker. Creating something from the ground up shows initiative, drive, and the ability to lead—qualities that scholarship committees are eager to support. If you've identified a gap or need in your community or industry, take action by creating a solution. Whether it's a nonprofit addressing social issues or a business tackling a unique problem, explain your motivation and the impact you've made.

7. Win Competitions or Tournaments – Prove Your Excellence

Whether academic, artistic, or athletic, competitions are a chance to show your dedication and talent in a specific area. Competitions provide an objective measure of excellence, and your achievements in these areas prove that you have the determination and skill to succeed. Highlight any national, regional, or local competitions you've excelled in. Explain the competitions, your role, and the skills you gained or demonstrated throughout the process.

8. Engage in Creative and Artistic Endeavors – Show Your Creative Side

Creative projects and artistic pursuits demonstrate your ability to think outside the box. Creative work adds depth and originality to your application, whether it's writing, painting, designing, or performing. Creativity shows that you're not afraid to take risks, experiment, and innovate—all qualities that scholarship committees highly value. Share examples of your creative work and explain the inspiration behind them. Highlight the skills and new perspectives you gained through these projects.

9. Pursue Advanced Learning Opportunities – Go Beyond the Basics

Seeking advanced learning opportunities shows you are proactive, self-motivated, and driven to improve. This habit shows that you're not just a passive learner—you actively develop new skills. Enroll in advanced courses, certifications, or workshops that go beyond your school's curriculum. Highlight any specialized training or extracurricular learning experiences that make you stand out.

10. Network and Seek Mentorship – Build Relationships That Support You

Building connections with professionals and mentors in your desired career field can provide invaluable support, guidance, and strong recommendation letters. Networking can also lead to scholarships via professional networks. Contact professionals, professors, and leaders in your area of interest. Cultivate relationships by seeking advice, learning from others, and demonstrating your commitment to personal growth.

Crafting Winning Scholarship Essays – A Powerful Story

Writing a scholarship essay isn't just about answering the prompt—it's about telling your story. It's your chance to show who you are, what you believe in, and where you're headed. A well-crafted essay can set you apart from the competition and boost your chances of winning. Before you even start writing, make sure you fully understand the prompt. Scholarship committees ask specific questions to learn about your character, values, and goals. Your job is to uncover those themes and thoughtfully address them.

Mastering the Art of Deciphering the Prompt

1. **Isolate Core Themes:** Break down the prompt to understand its main themes. For example, a prompt on leadership might include subthemes like teamwork, problem-solving, or community service. Understanding these layers will help you craft a more complete response.

2. **Engage in Reflective Brainstorming:** Reflect on personal experiences that align with the prompt's themes. These experiences don't have to be monumental. They can be small, everyday moments that show resilience, leadership, or growth.

3. **Tailor Your Experience:** Choose the experience that best fits the prompt and demonstrates your abilities. Be specific and focus on details that illustrate your growth and development, keeping the essay within the word count.

Writing the Essay – Building Your Narrative

Once you understand the prompt, it's time to start crafting your story. A scholarship essay must be clear, well-structured, and personal. It should show who you are beyond your grades and extracurricular activities.

1. **Craft a Compelling Introduction:** The introduction is your chance to grab the reader's attention. Start with something that draws them in. Use a vivid description, and thought-provoking question, or a personal story. The introduction sets the tone for the rest of your essay, so make it engaging.

   Example: *"On the podium, trembling before my peers, I realized public speaking wasn't just about delivering a speech. It was about overcoming my fear of failure."*

2. **Develop a Clear Structure:** Your essay should have a logical flow from start to finish. Make a clear beginning, middle, and end. Ensure each paragraph transitions smoothly to the next. You must also make your ideas easy to follow. Then, build them into a strong conclusion.

   Pro Tip: Connect your ideas using transitions like "As a result of this experience …" or "This led me to realize …"

3. **Show, Don't Tell:** Don't just tell the committee about your strengths (e.g., "I'm a hard worker"). Show them with concrete examples and descriptive stories. Let them see your work ethic and determination in action.

   Instead of "I'm a problem solver," write: *"During my internship, I found inefficiencies in our workflow. I then implemented a new system that cut processing time by fifteen percent."*

4. **Highlight Your Unique Voice:** Your personality should shine through your writing. Avoid writing in a way that feels artificial or overly formal. Authenticity is key—show the committee what makes you unique and how your values align with their mission.

   Example: *Instead of saying, "I want to help people,"* write: *"Having grown up in a close-knit community, I've always been driven by the desire to lift others up, whether through volunteer work or small acts of kindness."*

5. **Reflect and Connect:** Reflection is critical. It's not enough to share an experience; you need to connect it with the lessons you learned and how they will shape your future. Explain how the scholarship will help you achieve your goals.

Example: *"Overcoming my fear of public speaking has made me realize that every challenge is an opportunity for growth. This scholarship will allow me to pursue my dream of becoming an advocate for those without a voice."*

6. **Conclude with Impact:** Your conclusion should leave a lasting impression. Summarize your key points and reiterate why you're an excellent fit for the scholarship. Tie everything back to your future goals and show how the scholarship will help you achieve them.

   Example: *"Receiving this scholarship will enable me to continue my journey of personal growth and give me the tools needed to make a lasting impact on my community."*

7. **Polishing Your Essay – Perfecting the Details:** After writing your first draft, it's time to refine and polish your essay. Editing is essential to ensure your message is clear, concise, and compelling.

Revise and Edit: Set your essay aside for a day or two, then revisit it with a fresh set of eyes. Look for areas where you can improve clarity or strengthen your narrative. Remove unnecessary words or phrases that don't contribute to your story.

Seek Feedback: Ask teachers, mentors, or peers to review your essay and provide feedback. A fresh perspective can highlight areas you missed that need improvement.

Proofread Carefully: Before submitting your essay, proofread it meticulously. Check for grammar, spelling, and punctuation errors. Ensure your essay follows all the formatting guidelines and stays within the word count.

Sample Scholarship Prompt and Response Breakdown

Prompt: *"The lessons we take from obstacles we encounter can be fundamental to later success. Recount a time when you faced a challenge, setback, or failure. How did it affect you, and what did you learn from the experience?"*

Effective Response Example: Challenge – Overcoming Fear of Public Speaking

- **Introduction:** Start with an anecdote that sets the stage for the challenge.
- **Paragraph 1:** Describe the struggle and the emotional impact.
- **Paragraph 2:** Detail the actions you took to overcome the challenge.
- **Paragraph 3:** Reflect on the lessons learned and how they shaped your future goals.
- **Conclusion:** Connect the experiences to your long-term goals. Show how the scholarship will help you achieve those goals.

Why This Works: This response shows personal growth, action taken to overcome the challenge, and deep reflection on how the experience has shaped the applicant's future. It's specific, detailed, and related to the prompt's theme.

Chapter 9 Workbook

1. Types of Scholarships

Which type of scholarship—merit-based, need-based, community service, or field-specific—best fits your strengths and situation?

_____

_____

_____

_____

_____

2. Local Scholarships

What local scholarships are available? Ask your school's guidance counselor and consider community organizations and local businesses.

_____

_____

_____

_____

_____

3. Scholarship Search Engines

Explore scholarship search engines such as Fastweb or Scholarships.com. What scholarships did you find that match your strengths, interests, or academic goals?

_____

_____

_____

_____

_____

4. Diversifying Your Applications

List the types of scholarships you plan to apply for (e.g., local, national, field-specific).

_____

_____

5. Making Your Essay Powerful

Based on the "Powerful Approaches for Winning Scholarships" section of the book, how will you make your essays stand out from the competition?

_____

_____

_____

_____

_____

_____

_____

_____

_____

_____

6. Editing Your Essay

What steps will you take to ensure your essays are polished and error-free? Who can you ask to proofread your essays before submitting them?

_____

_____

_____

_____

_____

7. Choosing Recommenders

Who are the best people to write your scholarship recommendation letters? How well do they know your academic or personal achievements?

_____

_____

_____

_____

_____

Chapter 10: Education Benefits for Veterans

Thank you to those who have served, are serving, and will serve our nation. While many students will not qualify for the GI Bill, be commissioned by ROTC, or graduate from a service academy, all of the above can be a great way to pay for some or potentially all college expenses. For those returning to civilian life after serving our country, the GI Bill can be an excellent tool to help you acquire the qualifications you need to pursue new work opportunities. This chapter will guide you through the basics of ROTC, service academies, different versions of the GI Bill, and maximizing your benefits.

The Reserve Officers' Training Corps (ROTC)

ROTC pays for some or all of a student's college expenses. In return, the student commits to additional requirements while in college and serving in the armed forces after graduation.

Benefits: Beyond tuition assistance and a monthly stipend, ROTC programs provide valuable leadership training that can help students prepare for their roles in the armed forces and, eventually, the civilian workforce. With increased leadership experience, candidates can often secure better jobs. Another significant benefit is that officers and staff in the armed forces help mentor ROTC candidates.

Additional Commitments While in College: In addition to standard academic coursework, ROTC candidates must take various additional courses. They must also train for and pass challenging physical fitness tests. Commitments may include military science/history courses, other relevant subjects, leadership labs, field training exercises, and social events. Furthermore, ROTC cadets are required to follow uniform, grooming, and self-conduct standards. As a result of these additional commitments, ROTC students usually have less free time than their peers.

Commitments After College: Commitments can vary by school and ROTC program; however, students must typically serve between three and eight years. Service is often active duty, reserves, or a combination of both.

Eligibility:
- Be a US citizen.
- Be at least 17 and under 31 when commissioning.
- Have a high school diploma or equivalent.
- Self-report your high school unweighted Cumulative Grade Point Average.
- Provide your College Board scores (SAT or ACT).
- Identify up to 7 schools you are interested in attending.
- Provide your guidance counselor's and high school PE coach's email addresses.

To Learn More: Talk to your school's academic advisors and ROTC recruiters.[16]

Service Academies

An option for students looking to become officers or higher-level leaders in the armed forces is to apply to a service academy.

Curriculum and School Experience: Students can choose from a set of majors and must take classes to earn their chosen bachelor of science degree. To prepare for future service roles, students must also take technical and professional development courses related to their branch of the armed forces. While in school, students live in military barracks and wear uniforms. Like a traditional college, extracurricular activities, including sports, clubs, and social events, are also part of the educational experience.

Physical Training: Students undergo basic training over the summer before starting their first year of classes. While in school, they participate in daily military training. During the summer between academic semesters, they receive specialized training.

Rank: Students enrolled at a service academy are considered to be on active duty and are given the rank of midshipman (navy) or cadet (air force and army).

Tuition: Military academies generally do not charge tuition; students may even earn a salary or receive a stipend while attending.

Commitment: Students must complete a service requirement similar to that of ROTC programs. However, because military academies are more intensive, the service requirement may be higher than that of ROTC programs.

Requirements to Apply to a Military Academy

- Be a US citizen.
- Meet physical and medical requirements.
- Pass an interview.
- Apply for a nomination from your congressional representative or senator.
- Have a strong GPA and test scores.
- Demonstrate leadership potential.
- Show commitment to extracurricular activities, community involvement, and athletics.

Pros of Service Academies Compared to ROTC

1. **Better Financial Coverage:** Service academies cover tuition, room, board, and other expenses. ROTC, by comparison, often covers fewer costs.

---

[16] US Army. (n.d.). "*ROTC scholarships.*" goarmy.com. https://www.goarmy.com/careers-and-jobs/find-your-path/army-officers/rotc/scholarships.

2. **Immersive Military Environment and More Advanced Training:** Service academies provide a far more immersive, structured, comprehensive, and high-level training environment than ROTC programs.

3. **Faster Commissioning:** Military academies offer commissions upon graduation. ROTC candidates may need to complete more training and wait to be commissioned.

4. **Guaranteed Career Path:** Military academies provide a guaranteed career path and service requirement upon graduation.

5. **A Strong Network and Prestige:** Military academies can be a place to bond with peers and join a high-profile institution's alumni network. The degree and alumni connections will help you obtain future opportunities in the armed forces and civilian life.

Cons of Service Academies Compared to ROTC

1. **Less Flexibility:** Military academies are incredibly strict. Daily routines are, for the most part, determined for you, not by you. As a result, there is less personal and social freedom compared to being in an ROTC program. There is also no way to graduate from most programs early.

2. **Stricter Admissions Requirements:** ROTC programs are far easier to get into than military academies. Academies have highly competitive admissions processes that consider academic, physical, and leadership experience.

3. **Longer Service Obligation:** Academies invest far more resources in students and, as a result, demand a longer commitment than ROTC.

4. **Limited Academic and Extracurricular Choices:** Because academies are focused on preparing candidates for service in the armed forces, there are usually fewer academic and extracurricular options. So, a service academy may not be the best fit for students seeking a diverse educational experience.

5. **Demanding Education:** Academies push students hard, both physically and mentally, to prepare them for challenging leadership roles in the armed forces. Students who are not used to intense physical and mental demands may become overwhelmed.

Consequences of Not Finishing Your Requirements

If you don't meet your service requirement, fail out, or are kicked out of an ROTC or service academy program, you will be expected to pay back everything you have received. Many of these programs have zero-tolerance policies for bad behavior and test for drug use, so make good choices that help you reach your goals.

Montgomery GI Bill (MGIB)

Active Duty (MGIB-AD): This version is for active-duty members and veterans who meet specific criteria. It provides up to 36 months of benefits for college, vocational training, and apprenticeships.

- Service Requirements: At least 2 years of active duty with an honorable discharge.
- Education: High school diploma or GED.
- Contribution: Paid $1,200 during the first year of active service.
- Benefit Usage: Must use benefits within 10 years after leaving active duty.

Post-9/11 GI Bill

The Post-9/11 GI Bill covers up to 100% of in-state tuition and fees at public colleges. It can also provide a monthly housing allowance and a books and supplies stipend. Veterans who served after September 10, 2001, and their dependents may be eligible.

Tuition and Fees: Covers up to 100% of in-state tuition at public institutions. For private or foreign schools, there is a national cap on coverage.

Monthly Housing Allowance: Like the military's basic allowance for housing, this stipend is based on the local cost of living where the school is located.

Books and Supplies Stipend: Provides up to $1,000 each year to cover the cost of books and other educational materials.

Transferability: You can transfer unused GI Bill benefits to a spouse or children if you meet certain conditions, such as service obligations.

Service Requirement: At least 90 days of service after September 10, 2001. Or thirty days of continuous service if discharged due to a service-connected disability. Typically, three years of service is required to obtain full benefits.

Maximizing Your GI Bill Benefits

If you're a veteran or have a family member who served, the GI Bill may be able to help finance your education. Research your eligibility and the benefits you can access.

Use the GI Bill Comparison Tool: This tool, available on the Veterans Affairs website, can help you. It checks your eligibility, compares benefits, and finds VA-approved schools and programs for your education.

Choose the Right School: Many schools participate in the Yellow Ribbon Program, which helps cover additional tuition costs not covered by the GI Bill. This program is especially useful if you attend a private or out-of-state public institution.

Consider Online Programs: Online programs offer flexibility if you are balancing work or family commitments. The GI Bill covers many online degree and certification programs, allowing you to pursue education at your own pace.

Explore Nontraditional Programs: In addition to traditional college degrees, the GI Bill covers vocational training, apprenticeships, and certification programs. This gives you the option to pursue a wide range of career paths.

Utilize Career Counseling and Support Services: Many schools offer veterans career counseling, job placement, and mental health support to help them transition from military service to civilian jobs and education.

Lesser-Known GI Bill Benefits

Tutorial Assistance: Struggling with a particular subject? The GI Bill provides up to $1,200 for tutoring services, helping you stay on track academically.

Licensing and Certification Tests: If your career requires specific licensing or certification exams, the GI Bill can cover the cost of those tests.

National Testing Programs: Planning to take the SAT, GRE, LSAT, or GMAT? Your GI Bill benefits can be used to cover the cost of these entrance exams.

Work-Study Program: The VA's work-study program lets you earn money while in school. You can work in jobs related to veteran services, like at a VA hospital or a veterans center on campus.

Out-of-Pocket Expenses

While the GI Bill provides significant financial assistance, be mindful of possible out-of-pocket costs and create a plan to manage your budget effectively.

Monthly Housing Allowance: This stipend varies based on your school's location and whether you are a full-time or part-time student. It is also worth noting that the more dependents you have, the more money you will receive for this stipend. Be sure to budget accordingly, especially in areas with a high cost of living.

Out-of-Pocket Costs for Tuition: If you attend a private or out-of-state school or take more than the standard number of credit hours, your tuition may exceed the GI Bill's coverage. The Yellow Ribbon Program can help. Do your research and create a budget that factors in your GI Bill benefits, housing allowance, and other sources of income. Ensure your budget covers all living expenses so you remain financially secure.

How to Apply for GI Bill Benefits

1. **Determine Your Eligibility:** The VA website has a GI Bill Comparison Tool. You can use it to check your eligibility and explore participating schools.

2. **Gather Necessary Documents:** Collect service records, transcripts, and any required information.

3. **Submit an Application:** Complete VA Form 22-1990 (Application for VA Education Benefits) via the VA's eBenefits portal or mail it directly to the VA.

4. **Receive Your Certificate of Eligibility (COE):** Once your application is approved, you'll receive a COE. You must give it to your school's Veterans Affairs office.

5. **Enroll in a Program:** Choose a VA-approved school. Then, work with the Veterans Affairs office to certify your enrollment and ask for any tips they have to help you out.

Notes:_____

_____

_____

_____

_____

_____

_____

_____

_____

_____

_____

_____

_____

_____

_____

_____

_____

_____

_____

_____

Chapter 10 Workbook

1. Joining ROTC or a Service Academy

Do you think joining ROTC or a service academy would be a good choice for you? Why or why not?

_____

_____

_____

_____

_____

_____

2. Eligibility Criteria

Are you or a family member eligible for the GI Bill? If so, which version of the GI Bill applies to your situation? Or what service requirements must be met to qualify for these benefits?

_____

_____

_____

_____

_____

3. Using the GI Bill Comparison Tool

Visit the Veterans Affairs website and use the GI Bill Comparison Tool. Check your eligibility. Then, find schools in the Yellow Ribbon Program. What schools or programs best align with your educational goals?

_____

_____

_____

4. If Applicable, What Strategies from This Chapter Will You Use?

_____

_____

_____

_____

Chapter 11: Success in College and Life

College: The Modern-Day Epic Journey

College can be a great adventure if you plan and prepare for it. Unfortunately, many students and their families rush into the college process without enough planning or preparation. This often leads to problems that increase the risk of students struggling and dropping out. In this chapter, we'll explore the main reasons students drop out. Next, we will cover the four keys to college success. These keys will help you prepare for the challenges that cause most students to drop out.[17] However, we want to be clear that college planning and preparation isn't a one-time task. It is an ongoing effort. Olympians don't just train once and then stop. They constantly work on their mental, emotional, and physical fitness to prepare for competition. You, too, need to prepare, make a solid plan, and adapt continuously to set yourself up for massive success in college.

Reasons Why Students Drop Out of College

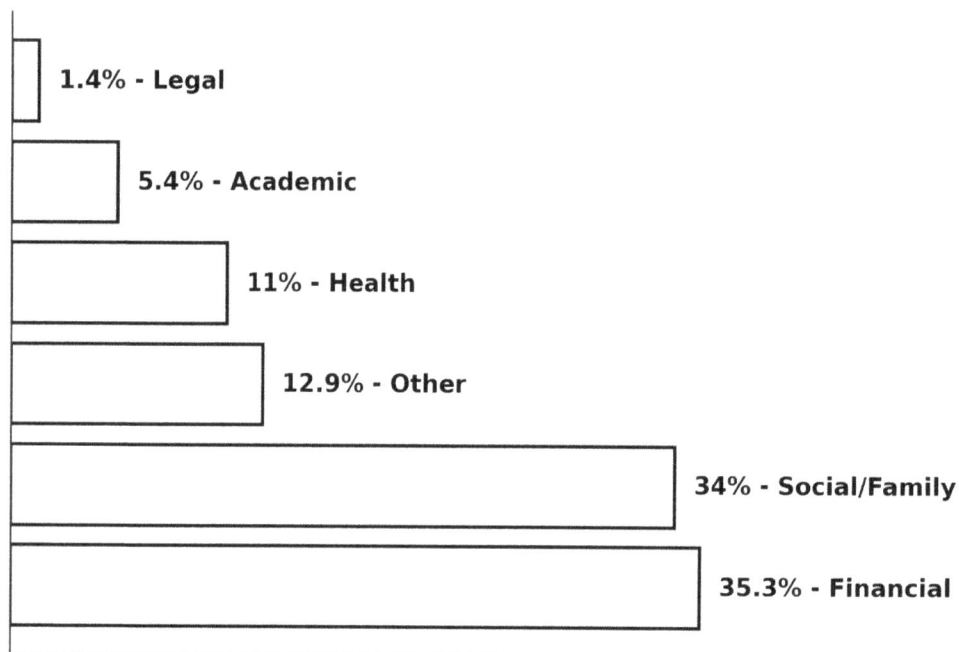

1.4% - Legal

5.4% - Academic

11% - Health

12.9% - Other

34% - Social/Family

35.3% - Financial

---

[17] LendEDU. (2017). College dropouts & student loan debt. *LendEDU*.

Control the Controllable

One of the most important lessons we can learn is that almost everything in life is beyond our control. We cannot control where we come from, the family we were born into, how much money we start with, or the body we were born with. However, we have 100% control over what we will do to honor the amazing gift of life entrusted to us. Many people have done something meaningful with their lives despite facing far harder financial, social, or health-related challenges than you or we face today. Find that person, even if they are a historical figure, and look up to them as an example. Learn from what they did and think about what you can do to achieve great results. For instance, if you lack resources, be resourceful, improvise, and adapt. If things are hard, keep your head held high and don't give up. You can take care of your mental and physical health and learn how to manage your finances. So, with all the things we can't control, let's control what we can.

Financial Reasons – 35.3% Dropout Rate

Financial struggles make college harder, no doubt about it. However, students have succeeded despite these challenges for generations and will continue to succeed for generations to come. In fact, students from tougher backgrounds often develop skills like work ethic, thrift, and creativity that more privileged students often lack. These qualities give students with a harder start unique advantages that money can't buy.

Take Robert, Marshall's grandfather, for example. He grew up dirt poor in Texas, going barefoot in the summer because his family could not afford shoes. He worked incredibly hard as a young man. He stayed longer than every other student in the classroom and worked on farms in the extreme summer heat. Eventually, he not only graduated but also earned a PhD in physics and worked on cold fusion. Though he never made much money as a professor, he and his wife saved every penny, stayed debt-free, donated to the causes they believed in, and sent all five of their kids through private schools and higher education. Their hard work paid off and significantly impacted not just their lives but those of their children, grandchildren, and great-grandchildren. The next chapter is all about saving money for college. So, don't worry, you'll get some great strategies.

Social and Family Reasons – 34% Dropout Rate

Homesickness, family issues, and a lack of social support make academics far harder. In college, you may feel alone at times. In those moments, your determination and a great team of people supporting you will make all the difference. Building a support system for yourself is crucial. Whether it's friends, family, or mentors, surround yourself with people who have your back. Ensure your supporters know your needs and what you are going through so they can best help you. It may also be worth taking advantage of the professional therapy services offered by many schools and insurance plans. Therapy is especially beneficial when discussing more private challenges you may feel uncomfortable sharing with friends and family.

Health Reasons – 11% Dropout Rate

Health challenges, whether physical or mental, are another major factor in student dropout rates. When students face serious health issues, it can be hard to keep up with the demands of college life. If you are struggling with a physical and/or mental health challenge, we sincerely feel for you and encourage you to seek professional support. Because physical and mental health are so critical, Chapter 13 is devoted to those topics.

4 Keys for College Success

1. Continuously Develop Compelling, Clear, and Concrete Goals.
2. Start Positive Habits and Break Bad Ones.
3. Develop the Right Tribe.
4. Focus on Your Primary Goal and Ignore What Others Think.

1. Continuously Develop Compelling, Clear, and Concrete Goals

You need to figure out what you want to accomplish with your one amazing life. Then, set powerful goals that will motivate you when things get hard. At first, your goals may be vague, but your task is to make them as clear as possible. Clarity will allow you to effectively plan and pursue your goals instead of becoming a victim of circumstance. The SMART goals system outlined below is a great way to set goals. Here is an example of how to use the system. Modify the example to meet your needs.

SMART Goals: Setting Goals You Can Achieve

If your main goal is to graduate college faster and with less debt, let's make it SMART: Specific, Measurable, Achievable, Realistic, and Time-Bound.

Specific: Decide how fast you want to graduate: in 2, 2.5, 3, 3.5, or 4 years. Consider your academic standing, transfer credits, and finances. Set a clear goal for your GPA and how much you aim to save by graduating early.

Measurable: Track your progress with measurable outcomes. Track how many credits you have completed and need to complete each semester to graduate on time. Monitor your GPA to ensure you stay eligible for accelerated programs. Review how much money you are saving by graduating early.

Achievable: Create a plan based on your strengths and weaknesses. It should be challenging but doable. If you struggle in a specific subject, factor in extra study time or tutoring.

Realistic: Set goals that challenge you but are still achievable. Aim to graduate in two or three years if possible, but take more time if needed. Consider limits, such as how many credits you can take per semester and how much time you have for your studies.

Time-Bound: Set deadlines for each milestone.

Pro Tip, Plan Backward: After you know your goal, you can plan backward. A simple example is trying to leave the house earlier. You would lay out your clothes, keys, phone, and other essentials the night before. This would make things quicker and easier in the morning. Use this same idea to make your big goals more attainable. Break up your big goals into the steps required to succeed. If your goal is to graduate in two or three years, what must you do each month, week, day, and hour to achieve that goal? What simple daily tasks, habits, and rules could help set you up for success? Also, how can you make the process as easy as possible so you follow through?

2. Start Positive Habits and Break Bad Ones

Good habits are foundational to success in any area of life, and college is no exception. Here are a few habits you should focus on to enhance your academic success.

Maximize Your Health: Good health plays a vital role in your performance as a student. College students are often surrounded by peers who frequently get sick, miss classes, and suffer burnout due to poor self-care habits. When pushing yourself to graduate early, every health setback can derail your progress. Missed classes, lost participation points, and feeling sick will all make your goals more difficult to achieve.

Prioritize your health through diet, exercise, and mental wellness. This will give you the energy and focus to thrive and avoid setbacks. Just don't be a hypochondriac!

Be a Voracious Learning Machine: College is a big investment. To maximize that investment, one must approach learning with enthusiasm and purpose. Relentless learners succeed in the classroom and beyond because they constantly seek knowledge that will give them more of an edge over the competition. Make it a habit to consume knowledge that will make you a standout performer in your future career. Read books. Listen to educational podcasts and audiobooks. Watch instructional videos. Best of all, get mentored by professionals in your field. We habitually listen to educational content while doing everyday tasks, like exercising, driving, and doing chores. This habit has improved our education far beyond what is taught in standard college classes, and we encourage you to try it.

Earn Your Teacher's Respect: Teachers notice which students value their lessons. Those same students who put in extra effort are more likely to get support, guidance, and letters of recommendation when needed. Not only are hardworking students setting themselves up for success, but teachers also want to see them succeed. Cultivate relationships with your teachers, especially those who are good mentors.

Ask for Help When You Need It: Never hesitate to ask for help. If you're struggling with coursework, balancing your schedule, or feeling overwhelmed, seek help from your friends, family, teachers, and school resources. When you demonstrate a willingness to work hard and improve, others will want to support you even more.

3. Develop the Right Tribe

Your social circle will heavily influence your success. As the saying goes, "You are the average of the five people you spend the most time with/compare yourself to." The same average effect applies to your education, job, wealth, health, and happiness. Surround and compare yourself with people who lift you up and challenge you to be better. In middle school and high school, we surrounded ourselves with friends who forced us to level up. Avoid those who engage in destructive behaviors and hold you back. In college, finding hardworking, intelligent friends who are strong in areas where you struggle is a game-changing strategy that will help you learn more and grow faster. If you help each other, you will have a wonderful, mutually beneficial friendship.

The Power of Quality over Quantity: A few close, trustworthy friends are better than many acquaintances. True friends are people you can count on; in return, they should be able to count on you. Don't be afraid to take as much time as you need to choose your tribe. You will be grateful later when those few solid friendships help you stay on track and grow. You will also create a powerful network to help you thrive in college and beyond by surrounding yourself with people who share your values and support your goals.

Am I a Good Friend? And Is This Friend Right for Me?

Don't just focus on finding great people; work to become a great friend to others. First, evaluate yourself and then your friends using the tough questions below. Improve your weak points and consider which friends you should spend more time with, less time with, and stop hanging out with completely.

- **Do they keep their commitments, or do they lack integrity?** Reliability and trustworthiness are essential for a healthy friendship.

- **Do they work as hard or harder than I do or lack drive?** It is important to surround yourself with people who are just as motivated as you are or more. Ambition is contagious, and so is sloth.

- **Are they respectful to others, regardless of their status or background?** A person's behavior toward others shows their character. This is especially true for how they treat those with less power or status.

- **Is the relationship mutually beneficial?** Friendships should involve equal give and take or, ideally, both sides always give as much as they can. If things are unbalanced, you will have future challenges with the relationship.

- **Do they have high work, health, and behavioral standards?** High standards in life reflect discipline and self-respect. Being around such people will challenge you to elevate your standards and way of life.

- **Do they engage in reckless behaviors like drug use?** Negative behaviors can be destructive not just to them but to everyone around them. Stay away from people who engage in or encourage dangerous activities.

- **How do I feel after spending time with them—energized or drained?** Friends should uplift you, not drain your energy. If you are consistently feeling worse after spending time with someone, that's a red flag.

4. Focus on Your Primary Goal and Ignore What Others Think

In college, you'll face social pressures and the temptation to follow the crowd. You can chase short-term highs, like alcohol, drugs, or casual relationships. But they will slow your progress. Staying focused is key to achieving your goals, so we have provided our best strategies below to help you keep your eyes on the ball.

Be Mindful of Drinking, Drugs, and Partying: Drugs and alcohol are major distractions. They steal your valuable time and health and are very risky. Marcus and I have seen the tragic effects of blackouts, overdoses, accidents, and deaths from alcohol and drug use. Chances are you have seen or heard of them too. College drinking and drug culture can be dangerous. It can lead to sexual assault, injury, or even death. The short-term high is not worth the long-term consequences. We would not tell you this if we did not live by the same standard. Neither of your coauthors was ever under the influence of alcohol or drugs during college.

Determine Your Focus: Identify your primary goal and put the majority of your energy into it. Whether it's graduating early, excelling academically, or fast-tracking your career, focus on what truly matters. Time is your most valuable asset. To reach the highest levels of success, you must use it wisely.

Long-Term, Find and Cultivate Your Passion: Find your passion and put your effort into that area. Don't waste time on fleeting distractions. Immerse yourself in what you love doing and surround yourself with like-minded people who support your growth. Achieving your goals and working on something meaningful is the most rewarding thing any of us can do with our limited time on this planet.

Notes:

_____

_____

_____

_____

_____

_____

Chapter 11 Workbook

1. College Preparation

College is hard. What will you do now to prepare for the challenges that will come so you can stay on course and graduate on time or early?

_____

_____

_____

_____

2. SMART Goals in Action

What SMART goal (Specific, Measurable, Achievable, Realistic, Time-Bound) can you set? It can be academic or personal. How will that goal help you in college?

_____

_____

_____

_____

_____

3. Navigating Financial Challenges

Many students drop out due to financial struggles. What strategies can you use to improve your finances and save on college expenses? Also, what big life skills/advantages can come out of experiencing financial hardship?

_____

_____

_____

_____

4. Building a Support System

What support system will you create to help you with challenges during college? Who can you turn to for support?

_____

_____

_____

_____

5. Better Health

What will you do today to become as healthy as possible, mentally and physically, to be ready for college?

_____

_____

_____

6. Defining Your Purpose

What is your primary purpose for attending college? How will staying focused on this purpose help you overcome challenges and stay motivated?

_____

_____

_____

7. Good Habits for Success

What habits do you currently have that can help you succeed in college? What bad habits currently hold you back, and how will you break them?

_____

_____

_____

8. Choosing Your Tribe

How can your friendships influence your success in college? What qualities do you look for in friends, and how can you become the kind of person others want as a friend?

_____

_____

_____

9. Purpose vs. Pleasure

How will you stay focused on long-term success rather than get caught up in distractions that will make it harder for you to achieve your goals?

_____

_____

_____

Chapter 12: Financial Tips for College

People often picture classrooms, dorms, and new friendships when they think of college. But behind the excitement of college lies a harsh reality. College is expensive, and we are not just talking about tuition. If you are unprepared, the costs will add up quickly and catch you off guard. Navigating college becomes far more challenging for students struggling with money. This is especially true when financial issues distract from academic priorities. Financial stress can significantly impact students' academic performance, mental health, and overall well-being. As you read earlier in this book, 35.3% of students who dropped out of college did so because of financial reasons. Understanding college expenses and how to manage them is one of the best ways to make college more manageable and enjoyable. We will show you how to prepare for college financially. Then, we will walk you through each expense step by step. This will help you control your college finances and stretch every dollar.

The Value of Hard Work – Making and Saving Money for College

We always tell young people to start making money and gaining work experience as early as possible. Working while being in school has major benefits. The biggest is often exploring careers and creating connections to help you get a better job after college. Working can also enable you to save money for college while learning the value of a dollar, work ethic, and self-reliance. Securing a job is a key step toward adulthood and should be celebrated. Gaining work experience is essential. But, school should come first unless finances demand otherwise. Look for part-time jobs that fit your schedule. Students typically work weekends, evenings, holidays, and summer breaks. Ensure that the work is safe, the environment is positive, and your coworkers have your back.

At some schools, you can get college credits for internships related to your future career. Marshall worked for his family's real estate management and investment company and earned several college credits. This can be a great way to get college credit while doing work you would have already done as part of a preexisting job or internship. Consider looking on your college's website and discussing options with your college's academic counselor if you feel this type of program would benefit you.

How Much You Could Save for College by Working Part-Time: If you are 16 and work ten hours per week at $15 per hour. Over two years (104 weeks), you'd earn about $15,600 before taxes and other expenses. Saving more would be better. But, if you set aside just one-third (33%) of your earnings, you'd have over $5,000. This money can help pay for expenses not covered by student loans. These include travel, food, supplies, and possibly housing. Additionally, if you continue to work just 10 hours a week at $15 per hour while attending two to four years of college, you could earn an additional $15,600 to $31,200. The financial benefits can be much more significant if you start saving earlier, earn higher wages, or work more hours.

Finding Work Under 16: This can be more challenging due to labor laws and since many businesses prefer older teens for liability reasons. Luckily, platforms like YouTube offer creative job ideas. Asking family, friends, neighbors, and local businesses you frequent can also provide great opportunities.

Family Contributions – Saving for College Together

Communicate openly with your family about the college process. Discussing costs helps set clear expectations and provides the information everyone needs to make smart financial decisions. Be upfront about who can help financially and how they will do so. Also, explore strategies, like a 529 plan or Coverdell education savings account.

529 College Savings Plan and Coverdell Education Savings Accounts: Both 529 plans and Coverdell ESAs are tax-advantaged savings plans that encourage families to save for future education expenses. Contributions grow tax-free, and withdrawals are tax-free if used for qualified education expenses, including tuition, room and board, school books, and fees.

- **State Tax Benefits:** Many states offer tax deductions or credits for contributions to a 529 plan, that can save you hundreds to thousands of dollars.
- **Flexibility:** Funds in a 529 plan or Coverdell Education Savings Account can be used for any eligible institution in the US and even some foreign schools. You can also change the beneficiary of either account type, allowing other family members to use the funds.

The Big Costs of College

1. Being Penny Wise, Pound Foolish

We want to ensure you don't end up paying a high price in the future by trying to save a little money today. For those of you who are just trying to make ends meet, we understand your options may be limited, but consider using the following ideas when possible. You only have one life, and trying to save money in a way that could dramatically reduce the length and/or quality of your life is unwise. For example, spending a bit more each day to eat healthy and exercise can add decades to your life and save you tens of thousands in medical bills. Plus, it will make life much more enjoyable. If no one is fit to drive, paying a little money for an Uber is a much safer choice than driving while impaired or being with an impaired driver. Drive the safest car you can afford. Don't try to save money by delaying car maintenance. Doing so is dangerous and shortens your car's life, costing more in the long run. Get frequent oil changes and replace your tires, brakes, battery, and other major parts well before they fail. When in doubt, spend the extra money to protect your health and safety.

2. Tuition Fees

When it comes to college expenses, tuition is usually the largest. But here's the thing: Tuition is not the same for all schools or students. Public schools charge less than private schools. In-state students pay less than out-of-state students. Nonprofit schools typically cost more than all other types of schools. Chapter 5 covers tuition costs in depth. If you want to find the best school and graduation strategy, look there. The key here is knowing the cost of tuition and being aware that tuition can increase yearly, so graduate faster if possible.

In-State Tuition – Save Thousands by Establishing Residency: Qualifying for in-state tuition at a public college is one of the best ways to save a ton of money. Out-of-state rates can be significantly higher. Establishing residency in your school's state can lower tuition costs in a big way. Residency requirements vary by state. Typically, students must live there for 12 months to establish residency. Each state and institution may have specific rules. So check your school's residency requirements. If you are already an in-state resident, you are ready to go. The following are key factors when considering residency requirements.

- **Living in the State:** You must physically reside in the state for the required period, typically at least one year.

- **Intent to Stay:** You need to demonstrate intent to remain in the state by obtaining a state driver's license, registering to vote, paying state taxes, or securing local employment.

- **Financial Independence:** Some states may require proof that you are financially independent, meaning your parents or guardians do not claim you as a dependent.

3. Room and Board – Where You Live Matters

Where you live can impact your budget. So, choosing between on-campus and off-campus housing is a big financial decision. Living with family is usually the cheapest option and will save you a lot of money. If that's not possible, living on campus is often the next best choice. It's convenient, safe, saves time, and lets you focus on studying to graduate early. You get a furnished dorm room, you're close to classes, and a meal plan saves time on food prep and cleanup. If off-campus living is your only option, don't worry—we've got solid tips to help you rent smart. We'll show you how to handle hidden costs and find the right roommates to split expenses with.

Choosing Off-Campus Housing: Renting an apartment takes careful planning. Many landlords expect you and your roommates to have a combined income of 3–5 times the rent. Or have enough cash in your bank account to cover the lease. This is a challenging qualification for most students to meet. A parental guarantor might be needed. But before you waste time and money, check if the complex accepts parental guarantees and can work with your finances. Landlords also run background and credit checks. A credit score below 650 could mean a bigger security deposit is required or even rejection, so check with management first. Usually nonrefundable and around $100 per person, application fees can add up fast. If money's tight, look for older independently run properties. They are usually more affordable, and management may be less strict when it comes to accepting applicants.

Fees and Hidden Costs of Leasing an Apartment: Unlike on-campus housing, which often has a single set price, renting off-campus comes with many hidden fees. Ask for a written breakdown of all the fees and estimated utility costs. This will help you understand the full cost of rent and compare different apartments. When possible, negotiate move-in specials, like a free month of rent and waived application fees.

Common List of Fees

Application Fees: $50–$100 per person (nonrefundable).

Security Deposit: Usually $500 to 2 months rent, but may be higher with poor credit.

Utility Deposits/Fees: Cost for water, electricity, gas, Internet, etc.

Pet Fees: Additional fees for pets. Often $400 one time and $25–$50 monthly.

Parking Fees: Monthly fees for parking spaces.

Move-In Fees: These are nonrefundable and charged by some apartment complexes.

Trash Fees: Charged monthly in some buildings.

Other Fees: Always ask for a complete list of all fees and costs. Determine pest control, amenity, common area, maintenance, and admin fees, among other things.

Utility Costs: Ask management for their best estimates on utility fees, such as power, water, sewer, and Wi-Fi. Depending on the area, these usually cost $100 to several hundred dollars monthly.

Roommates: Sharing Costs and Responsibilities

Roommates can cut your costs big time. You split rent, utilities, and sometimes household items. In his second year of college, Marshall moved off-campus with a roommate. This was due to an on-campus housing shortage. Renting an apartment was more expensive than living on campus. That said, Marshall saved about $1,000 a month by having a roommate compared to living alone. But living with a roommate comes with its challenges. Here are some tips to ensure you find a good fit.

Start early: The best potential roommates plan ahead. So, starting your search late limits your choices.

Be a desirable roommate: A reputation for cleanliness, responsibility, and hard work makes you a first-choice roommate.

Ensure financial stability: Your roommate should be able to cover their share of the rent and utilities. Confirm they have a guarantor and strong finances. Otherwise, you might have to pay for everything.

Commitment to college: Ensure your roommate is focused on graduating, not just on having fun. Uncommitted roommates can be distracting, and they may also stop paying rent if they drop out of school.

Compatibility: Find someone with a similar routine, values, and cleanliness standards. Compatibility will help you avoid most conflicts.

Set clear expectations: Write an agreement. It should cover who will pay for what costs and who will do which household tasks. Also, set guest rules and quiet hours.

4. Supplies

School and apartment supplies can add up quickly, but here are ways to save money.

Thrifting: Thrift stores can be an excellent source for buying college essentials. You can find furniture, cooking supplies, notebooks, and folders for a fraction of the price of buying them new.

School Buy-Sell Groups: Students are constantly coming and going. Looking at your school's online buy-sell groups can be a great way to find supplies at great prices. Remember to negotiate if the price of an item is too high.

Textbooks/Electronics: They can be ridiculously expensive. But you don't have to fall into the trap of paying full price. Here are some smart ways to cut down on costs.

- **Rent textbooks or buy used ones.** Don't pay full price if you don't have to.

- **You can check out online resources or use your school's library.** Most libraries have copies of the textbooks you need.

- **Go digital.** E-books and online versions can save you a ton of money. You may even find some textbooks for free on the Internet.

- **Share resources.** You can share login codes and books with your peers and split the costs.

- **Consider refurbished electronics.** Need a laptop? Look for refurbished models from trusted sellers like Apple, Amazon, or Best Buy. The savings are real, but do your research to ensure quality. Also, see if there are student discounts available. Apple has student discounts, so make sure to use them.

- **Resell your textbooks.** Take good care of your books and notes, then resell them to recoup some of the costs.

5. Transportation – Getting There and Back

Transportation costs depend on your college's location. The more remote the campus, the higher the transportation costs will be. You might not need a car if you live within walking distance of your classes and have shops nearby. Marshall saved thousands by skipping car ownership and using Uber instead. He did not have to pay for insurance, gas, maintenance, or parking fees. Uber or public transport is easier for most students than owning a car. Many schools offer discounted or even free public transportation or ride-sharing for students. Carpooling with friends can also help you save on gas and parking. Biking can be another great option; however, biking on major roads can be very dangerous. If your commute area has unsafe bike lanes or sidewalks, don't bike unless it's your only option. You only get one brain and body to last a lifetime. So, if you are biking, scootering, or riding a motorcycle, be cautious and wear a high-quality helmet that has not expired from age or damage. We strongly advise against motorized scooters with small wheels. Cracks or unevenness in the road can cause you to crash, and many people we know have broken arms and experienced severe injuries.

6. Health Insurance and Medical Expenses

Health insurance is usually mandatory when attending college. If your family's plan doesn't cover you, you'll likely have to pay for the school's plan or another plan that meets the requirements. If you're already insured, make sure you're not also paying for the school's plan because that is a big waste of money. If you need coverage, many schools offer cheap student health plans. But research them to ensure they meet your needs. Also, remember to factor in the costs of doctor and dentist visits, prescriptions, and over-the-counter meds.

7. Personal Expenses – The Silent Budget Killer

The little things add up, like laundry, phone bills, personal care items, and hanging out with friends. These might seem small, but over a year, they can significantly dent your budget. The key to managing personal expenses is to set a monthly budget and stick to it. Once you know how much money you can afford to spend, it is easier to make choices that help you get ahead financially.

8. Miscellaneous and Unexpected Costs

Life happens. Maybe your laptop breaks, or you must make an emergency trip home. These unexpected expenses can derail your budget if you're not ready for them. The solution? Have a financial cushion. Set aside some money for those "just in case" moments. You'll thank yourself later.

Spending Money in a Meaningful Way

Now that you understand the big and small costs you will face in college, consider this. Money can be spent in countless ways. However, if you want to live a prosperous life, money must be used purposefully. We want to ensure that you don't end up like an average American with huge debts and no savings. After all, it is easy to get into debt. Companies give out loans, and then ads and pop culture urge you to buy everything you can afford and many things you can't. Despite living in one of the wealthiest countries in the world, most Americans live paycheck to paycheck with no emergency savings.

Understand the Real Cost of Spending: Each dollar can have a positive, lasting impact if you use it to pay off debt or invest. For instance, a student loan at a 7% or 9% interest rate will cost about $1.70 to $1.90-plus for every dollar borrowed over ten years. This concept also applies to lost investment opportunities. You could reasonably expect to have $2 in ten years for every dollar invested today. Before buying something unnecessary, remember it costs about double over the next ten years. If you wouldn't pay double the price, it's probably not worth it.

Spend Money Where It Counts: Cut wasteful spending on subscriptions and unneeded things. Focus on what is truly valuable. Prioritize spending on what matters most rather than trying to impress others with flashy purchases. Use your money to:

1. **Pay down debts.**
2. **Invest in your future.**
3. **Improve your health.**
4. **Live life on your terms.**

Tips on Going Out Without Breaking the Bank

College students often overspend on food and drinks. Cutting back on nights out and finding low or no-cost social activities can save you thousands. For example, cutting weekly social spending from $100 to $50 could save you $2,600 a year. If money is tight and you are taking on debt to pay for school, save going out for special occasions.

- **Skip the drinks** and enjoy socializing without alcohol.
- **Find affordable restaurants** and use BOGO deals and app rewards from chain restaurants for discounts and free food.
- **Enjoy nature.** Parks, beaches, and hiking are often free or inexpensive.
- **Explore museums, theaters, aquariums, farms, and zoos.** Many offer free or discounted days for students and in-state residents.

Budgeting for Financial Success

A budget isn't meant to restrict you. Instead, it gives you control over your financial decisions. A clear budget lets you cut waste, save, and reach your financial goals.

Steps to Create a Budget:

1. **List Your Income:** Include all sources of income, such as part-time jobs, scholarships, and allowances.
2. **Track Your Expenses:** Write down every expense, no matter how small.
3. **Categorize Expenses:** Divide your expenses into categories like housing, food, transportation, entertainment, and savings.
4. **Set Goals:** Determine your financial goals, such as saving money for an emergency fund, paying off debt, and investing.
5. **Adjust Spending:** Compare your income and expenses. Adjust spending to ensure you live within your means and meet your financial goals.

How to Use Credit Cards to Improve Your Finances

Credit Cards and Credit Scores: Credit cards can be a powerful financial tool. They do require you to use discipline and responsibility to avoid accumulating debt. Credit cards offer several benefits when used wisely. They help you build your credit score, earn cash back, and get protection from fraud. This section will cover how credit cards work, their benefits, and how to use them responsibly for long-term financial health.

How Credit Cards Work

Credit vs. Debit Cards: A credit card lets you borrow money for purchases you must repay, while a debit card takes money from your bank account for purchases. Debit is like spending cash. If you don't pay your credit card bill by the due date, you'll be charged high interest rates, often 20% or more. This can lead to significant debt and financial instability.

Application Process: You can apply for a credit card after turning 18. Credit card companies will review your income, credit score, and other financial factors to decide whether to approve your application. For students with no credit history, look for companies that offer student credit cards and easier approval.

Credit Limit: If approved, you'll receive a credit limit, typically ranging from $500 to $1,500 for students with limited or no income. This is the maximum amount you can borrow on the card until you pay the balance off. Paying on time and in full each month will increase your credit limit and score over time.

Pay It Off in Full: Never spend more on your credit card than you can afford to pay off. Set up autopay. It will ensure you pay the full balance each month. This will help you avoid late fees and interest charges. Paying in full lets you stay debt-free while having fraud protection, earning rewards, and building your credit.

Benefits of Using a Credit Card Responsibly

1. **Cashback/Intro Bonuses:** Credit cards often offer **1%–3% cash back** on purchases. This means for every $100 you spend, you'll receive $1 to $3 back. However, ensure you're not paying additional fees to use the card, which can end up costing you more. When you sign up for a credit card and spend the required amount, you can often get intro bonuses, basically free cash, often $100 or more.

2. **Building Your Credit:** Paying your credit card on time each month builds your credit score. A good score is vital for helping you lease an apartment or get good terms when buying a car or getting a mortgage. A good credit score can save you thousands of dollars in interest over your lifetime by qualifying you for lower rates on loans.

3. **Credit Score:** Your credit score is a numerical representation of your creditworthiness. A higher score makes it easier to get loans and qualify for lower interest rates. Paying your credit card on time and keeping your balance low compared to your credit limit will improve your score over time.

4. **Fraud Protection:** Credit cards offer robust protection against fraud and theft that debit cards and cash do not. If your card is lost, stolen, or used without permission, you can contact the credit card company to resolve the issue. In comparison, you would be out of luck if a $100 bill were lost or stolen from your wallet.

Potential Credit Card Pitfalls: Avoiding Debt and Interest

High Interest Rates: If you don't pay off your balance in full, interest charges will accumulate, leading to big debts. For example, a $1,000 balance on a card with a 20% interest rate can quickly grow to $1,200-plus if not paid for a year. This is why it's crucial to pay the entire balance by the due date.

Overspending: Credit cards can tempt you to spend more than you can afford. Stick to a budget and only use your credit card for purchases you can pay off in full monthly.

Review all Charges: Every few days, make sure all the charges on your credit card are correct. This will help you spot and stop fraud. Regularly reviewing your expenses also enables you to budget more effectively by allowing you to see how much money you are spending and what costs you can reduce or cut completely.

"A penny saved is a penny earned."
– Benjamin Franklin, Founding Father of the United States

Chapter 12 Workbook

1. Part-Time Work for Savings

Imagine you start working part-time. How much could you save for college by the time you graduate, and how would you prioritize using that money?

_____

_____

_____

2. Family Contributions

Why is it important to have open conversations about paying for college with your family? If possible, can family members contribute to a college savings plan/account?

_____

_____

_____

3. Penny Wise, Pound Foolish

What are some ways you have tried to save money in the past that you won't do moving forward because, in the long run, they will end up costing you more?

_____

_____

_____

4. On-Campus vs. Off-Campus Housing

What do you think would be better for you living on or off campus, and why?

_____

_____

_____

5. Handling Hidden Housing Costs

Renting off-campus comes with hidden costs. How will you determine the full cost of renting? What additional strategies will you use to save money on housing?

_____

_____

_____

6. Roommates

What qualities will you look for in a good roommate?

_____

_____

_____

7. Cutting Personal Expenses

What personal expenses, like entertainment or outings with friends, add up for you? How will you budget to control costs while still enjoying your college experience?

_____

_____

_____

8. Unexpected Costs

What unexpected costs might you face in college or have you faced in the past? How will you prepare for these potential expenses?

_____

_____

_____

9. Spending Money Meaningfully

What is the best use of your money to help you achieve your goals?

_____

_____

_____

10. Using Credit Cards Responsibly

How can responsible credit card use build your credit score and save you money? What are the risks of using credit cards irresponsibly?

_____

_____

_____

Chapter 13: Mental and Physical Health

As you work toward fast-tracking your education and career, remember that good mental and physical health is the number one most important thing to build a foundation for a successful, fulfilling life. The strategies in this chapter will help you build robust health and provide a plan to maintain your health while facing the challenges of college.

The Challenge of College

College is mentally and physically tough, especially for those aiming to graduate early. As mentioned earlier, 11% of students drop out due to health issues. This even happened to a few of our peers. To succeed, you need stamina, resilience, and strong mental and physical health. This chapter will give you strategies to build those key attributes. Success isn't just about intelligence; it's about endurance. College is a marathon, not a sprint. Staying healthy will help you handle the workload and pressure for the long haul.

Evaluating Your Health Before College

Neither of your coauthors is a health care/medical professional or claims to be. Consider our advice to be coming from a friend who cares about you and is just offering their best ideas. Seeking professional help if you need it is not a sign of weakness. It is a proactive step that we highly recommend to increase your chances of success. Compare your health checkup to a racecar driver getting their car tuned up by a mechanic before a race. The tune-up improves their chances of winning and makes the race safer. Below is a personal mental health evaluation you can use. Work hard using the strategies in the pages ahead so you can confidently check off all the boxes. This will give you a strong mental health foundation to help you in college.

Personal Mental Health Evaluation

- Can I manage stress in positive ways?
- Do I have a strong support network and ask for help when needed?
- Am I adaptable in times of change and resilient in tough situations?
- Do I have good time management and organizational skills?
- Do I live a healthy lifestyle in terms of diet, sleep, and exercise?
- Do I focus on making progress rather than trying to make things perfect?
- Do I have a history of mental health concerns that I should pay attention to?

1. **The Two Ways to Deal with Stress:** Stress can motivate you to overcome challenges, but it can also lead to harmful behaviors like procrastination and addiction. Fight for your future. Manage stress by taking action, exercising, practicing mindfulness, and planning. Don't give in to unhealthy coping methods.

2. **Ask for Help, Find Support, and Give Back:** College can be tough. You may be far from home and have many responsibilities to deal with, so don't hesitate to ask teachers, peers, tutors, and mentors for help. Reach out to family and old friends who care about you and can provide much-needed support. Branch out by building new friendships and finding mentors who push you to get better. In Marshall's life, mentors, like his high school teacher Jesus Santos, played a huge role. He introduced Marshall to ultra-endurance sports and inspired him to write this book. Don't underestimate the power of therapy or professional guidance when facing complex issues. A mentor or therapist can help you work through challenges that family or friends may be unable to handle. It's worth mentioning again that many schools have advisors, mentors, and therapists you can meet with at little to no cost. Additionally, many insurance plans cover therapy and psychiatry. The last thing to remember is that many people will help you during your time in college. At the same time, many students will be struggling and need help, so give back by supporting others. Helping others will feel amazing and make your campus a much happier and friendlier place to be. A smile, kind words, or simply listening can make a huge difference in someone else's day and yours.

3. **Be Resilient and Adaptable:** College is full of challenges that require you to be resilient and adaptable. You must handle heavy workloads, adapt to a new environment, and be ready for new experiences. Work on becoming more resilient and adaptable so you can navigate college more effectively and emerge stronger from the challenges you will face. To accomplish this, we recommend that you take on a mental/physical challenge that will force you to grow as a human being. For example, running a marathon or learning a challenging and valuable new skill.

4. **Time and Resource Management:** Time and resource management are vital. Doing so will help you experience less stress and achieve your goals. You must balance your schoolwork, social life, and personal well-being to maximize productivity and minimize overwhelm.

5. **Healthy Living, Healthy Mind:** A healthy lifestyle with a good diet, exercise, and sleep is fundamental for mental health. A well-nourished, well-rested body leads to a sharper, more resilient, and healthy mind.

Diet: A diet high in fruits, vegetables, and lean proteins can boost your mood and energy.

Exercise: Regular weekly exercise for at least 150 minutes boosts mood and reduces depression. Do not think of it as a chore, either. Find ways to exercise that you enjoy. Try running, weightlifting, swimming, walking, or other sports. Just get up and get moving.

Sleep: Aim for 7–9 hours of sleep per night to give your body and mind time to recharge and heal.

6. **Having Clear Goals and the Ability to Persevere:** A big goal ignites your soul. It pushes you to keep going, even when times are tough, plans fail, and setbacks occur. Use the

SMART goals framework. Set a goal that is powerful enough to change your life and keep you motivated even when times are tough. Be specific. Maybe you want to graduate in two years and save tens of thousands of dollars to build a better life for yourself and your loved ones. Anticipate setbacks and see them as opportunities to grow, not reasons to quit. When a plan fails, don't just bounce back—come back stronger, wiser, and more determined to succeed.

7. **Addressing Past Mental Health Challenges:** If you've struggled with mental health in the past, put extra effort into maintaining good habits and seeking professional support when necessary. College is an opportunity to strengthen your mental health by adopting positive behaviors and managing stress effectively.

Getting Professional Help: Maintaining mental and physical health sometimes requires professional assistance. Here's an overview of what to look for in a mental health professional.

- **Psychiatrists:** Look for a psychiatrist who focuses on holistic care, not just medication. A psychiatrist should work with patients on lifestyle factors, including diet, exercise, and sleep.

- **Therapists:** A therapist can help you work through personal challenges. Find someone who shares your values and pushes you to grow. Don't settle for comfort—choose someone who challenges you to do the hard personal work.

Physical Health: The Foundation for Success

1. **Evaluating Your Physical Health:** Many people have succeeded in college despite disabilities and health issues. It's best to be in excellent health before starting college. But that's not always possible. If you have a disability or chronic condition, planning ahead is key. Set up accommodations, medical plans, and support systems with the school before you begin. If you have ongoing health challenges, be extra mindful about your health because bacteria and viruses spread fast on college campuses. Most schools require a physical. So, take this chance to address your health concerns with your doctor.

2. **Are You Fit?** Fitness is a big key to your success in college. Being fit has more than just physical benefits. It helps you better handle stress, uncertainty, and challenges. Being in good shape boosts your energy, mood, and ability to fight off illnesses. Fitness enhances your college life, making walking with a heavy backpack or participating in active extracurricular activities easier. Plus, studies show that regular exercise combats depression and anxiety, which many college students face.

3. **The Importance of Sleep:** We cannot overstate the importance of sleep for mental and physical health. Sometimes, we had to sleep less than six hours a night in college. We don't recommend it, except for short periods to hit a big goal. There is a big price to pay for a lack of sleep, so don't push it. Many students stay up late partying, pull all-nighters, and rely on caffeine to keep going. However, under-sleeping and overuse of caffeine can lead to serious

health issues. We want to live long, healthy lives and not burn out in our twenties! I am sure you want the same thing for yourself! This is why we recommend saving caffeine for finals week or, better yet, avoiding it altogether. The FDA suggests 400 mg of caffeine is the safe upper limit, but once again, try to use as little caffeine as possible. If you use caffeine daily, it's time to reassess your sleep habits. Try the strategies below to boost your natural energy and cut back on stimulants.

Tips for Better Sleep in College:

- Find a roommate with a similar sleep schedule to minimize disruptions.
- Set a consistent bedtime and wake-up time to regulate your body's internal clock.
- Wind down before bed by avoiding screens and bright lights.
- Avoid alcohol, tobacco, and caffeine.
- If you work out your body and brain while chasing your goals, you will have no problem getting good sleep.
- Spend time outdoors in natural sunlight to help regulate your sleep cycle.
- Make your bed and sleeping area as comfortable as possible, and reduce light and noise for better rest.
- Avoid watching unsettling movies before bed.
- Don't use any blue light devices more than necessary.

4. **Fuel Up with Healthy Eating:** What we put into our bodies either builds our health or breaks it down. Excellent health makes life so much richer and more enjoyable. For that reason, we highly recommend choosing a school with healthy food options. If that's not possible, try to find ways to fuel yourself with whole foods. Consider buying and preparing food or using a meal prep service. Skip soda, sugary drinks, and processed foods as much as possible. Also, if you have dietary restrictions or allergies, ensure you can meet your needs while in school.

5. **Maintaining and Improving Your Physical Health:** In college, your goal should not be just to maintain your health but to improve it. Without parental oversight, it's on you to manage your health. This includes your medical conditions, medications, diet, exercise, and wellness. Exercise regularly, eat well, try yoga and meditation, and spend time outdoors. Many schools have fantastic exercise facilities and free yoga and meditation clubs/classes. Take full advantage of these amenities; you are paying for them with your tuition, after all. Another impactful thing to do is to surround yourself with health-minded people and stay committed to choices that support your long-term well-being. Also, check your school's health care options. Look into on-campus clinics, nearby pharmacies, and providers. Have a plan for medical care when needed, and don't skip preventive care like regular checkups.

One Body and One Mind for a Lifetime

We are all incredibly lucky to be alive. Countless things could have gone wrong along the way, yet here we are. With that gift comes the responsibility to care for ourselves—both body and mind—because we only get one of each to last a lifetime. In college, taking care of your physical and mental well-being is essential. How you treat yourself now will have lasting effects on your future health, happiness, and success. Treasure your body by nourishing it with healthy foods, regular exercise, and sufficient sleep. Safeguard your mind by managing stress, practicing self-care, and seeking help when needed.

"The person with health has a thousand wishes. The person without health has only one."

– Indian proverb

Notes:

_____

_____

_____

_____

_____

_____

_____

_____

_____

_____

_____

_____

_____

_____

_____

_____

_____

_____

Chapter 13 Workbook

1. Mental Health Check-In

What are some signs that you may need to seek support for your mental health? How can you create a plan for managing your stress and mental well-being?

_____

_____

_____

2. Stress Management Strategies

How do you typically respond to stress? What positive methods can you use to manage stress in college?

_____

_____

_____

3. Asking for and Giving Help

Who will you reach out to for help when you need it, and how can you help others?

_____

_____

_____

4. Resilience and Adaptability

How can building resilience and adaptability help you better navigate the challenges of college?

_____

_____

_____

5. Healthy Lifestyle Habits

How will you implement a healthy diet to improve your mental and physical health during and after college?

_____

_____

_____

6. Maximizing Fitness in College

What fitness activities do you enjoy? How can you fit them into your busy schedule to boost your energy, mood, and academic performance?

_____

_____

_____

7. The Importance of Sleep

Because sleep greatly impacts your mental and physical health, what strategies can you use to ensure you get enough sleep?

_____

_____

_____

8. Energy Management vs. Caffeine

What are some natural ways to boost your energy and focus throughout the day instead of relying on caffeine?

_____

_____

_____

9. Seeking Professional Help

If you're facing mental or physical health challenges, what steps will you take to address them? Consider making a therapist, psychiatrist, or doctor part of your plan if possible.

_____

_____

_____

10. Long-Term Health Goals

How much better would you feel and look if you created and maintained positive mental and physical health habits for a lifetime?

_____

_____

_____

Chapter 14: Life Skills to Help You Succeed

How Will You Choose to See the World?

Everyone will face difficulties, challenges, and tragedies in life. However, you can control how you interpret those events, and your interpretations will determine the quality of your life. When things get hard, you can get scared. Or you can be confident in your amazing abilities as a member of the human race to find a solution to every challenge. After all, as Tony Robbins, the motivational speaker and author, is known for saying, "Life happens for us, not to us." Every challenge we confront offers us the chance to become a better version of ourselves. Adopting this empowering perspective will transform your life and make the strategies in this book ten times more effective. We just discussed the number one life skill: a powerful mindset. Now, let's cover additional life skills that will help you be successful in college and beyond.

Creating Structure

Creating structure boosts productivity and supports mental and physical health, which are both key factors to your academic success. Students who stick to a solid schedule consistently outperform their peers. The best way to build structure is by creating a daily/weekly routine and sticking to it. Here's a great way to start.

1. **Class Times:** Build your schedule around class times and school commitments. You can often pick class times and structure your classes around your needs in college.

2. **Wake-Up and Sleep Times:** Set a consistent time to wake up and go to bed. You can use your iPhone's bedtime feature.

3. **Workout Times:** Find the best time to work out. We recommend early morning—it's a great way to start the day, guarantees you get it done, and the gym is less crowded.

4. **Meal Times:** Set regular meal times and avoid eating late at night for better health.

5. **Study and Work Times:** Block time for studying and work if you have a job.

6. **Fun/Social Time:** Schedule time to hang out with positive people and have fun. Even during busy times, you can catch a quick meal at the school cafeteria or study together. Finishing work early in the semester will also free up more time and reduce your stress.

Planning

Using a paper and digital planner helps you stay organized and on track with assignments, tests, and personal responsibilities. Plan out your entire semester before the first day of class by looking at all course syllabi and writing out all the due dates and test dates. You can also adjust and add to them as needed. This ensures you're not caught off guard by deadlines or exams. Planning was one of the biggest factors in our success throughout school. Without our planners, we would have forgotten countless assignments and missed studying for tests. Paper planners are amazing because everything is right in front of you and is a constant reminder of what you need to tackle next. Digital calendars are also key because they provide additional redundancy and reminders. We recommend using a paper and a digital system, so you always have a backup. Plus, digital tools on Google are perfect for sharing during group projects.

Tips for Using a Planner

1. **Set Two Dates:** For each assignment, mark two dates—one for when you'll start working on it and one for when it's due. Give yourself plenty of time to finish ahead of the deadline.

2. **Start with the Big Tasks:** Prioritize the biggest, most important tasks first. Then, fit the smaller tasks around them, not the other way around.

3. **Use Color:** Some people use different colors for different classes or tasks to stay organized.

4. **Personal and School:** Use your planner for both personal and school tasks. Divide it into sections to keep it clean.

5. **Plan the Whole Semester Before Day 1:** At the start of each semester, fill out your planner. Add in all assignment deadlines, test dates, personal plans, and important events. It's much more efficient than checking the syllabus. However, be ready to change due dates or add assignments if things change.

6. **Setting Reminders:** Reminders are key to staying on track and not missing classes or meetings. Set two alerts on your phone: one an hour before and another 30 minutes before. This ensures you show up early and don't forget your commitments.

Time Management: Getting Ahead of Deadlines

Procrastination is the downfall of many students. People create a ton of unnecessary stress by procrastinating on schoolwork. The result is all-nighters, poor-quality work, and relying on caffeine to stay awake. If you want to graduate early, especially in two years, you need a better approach. Our strategy was to knock out as many assignments as possible at the start of every semester. This gave us more time to focus on big projects and exams and have fun later in the semester. The result was better performance and less stress. We even asked professors to allow us to finish future assignments so we could work ahead. Easy points can be earned from homework, attendance, and participation. Finishing work early keeps you on track and reduces mistakes. Stay ahead, and you'll outperform the majority of students.

Time for Relaxing and Friends

We want to be honest with you. The harder you work to graduate early and set yourself up for a successful career, the less time you will have to relax or socialize. This is the price you will pay, but I promise you that in the long run, it will be worth it if you follow a few key strategies to avoid burnout and make the process more fun.

1. **Find Joy in the Challenge and Know Your Why:** Graduating college early is tough. We will keep saying this because we want you to be ready for the challenge. By far, the best advice we can give you to avoid burnout is to find joy in working through the obstacles standing between you and your goals. After all, life is "about the climb." We make hard things into a game so they are more fun. For example, we tried to see how far in advance we could get work done for a class and how fast we could do it. We also tried to be the best students in our class, win competitions, and receive top scores on tests and assignments. Whatever work you are doing, try to find a way to make it into a fun, silly game that no one but you will ever understand. Sometimes, things will just be hard and feel unbearable. In those moments, you will need to remember why you are working so hard and never forget it. As long as you hold that reason in your heart, you will be able to keep moving forward. For motivation/inspiration, check out the poems "Man in the Arena," "The Will to Win," and "Invictus."

2. **Find Friends for the Challenge Who Support You:** Writing this book has been hard. But doing it with a team of great people has made the process fun and the book's quality far higher. If you want to be successful, find friends who will push you, encourage you, and have fun with you while you are working hard together. Try to schedule classes together so you can work as a team on assignments. You won't have much time for socializing when taking lots of courses, so eat, exercise, and study with friends. This will help you make the most of your limited time to socialize. After all, every college student needs to eat and study.

3. **Focus on Quality over Quantity with Goals, Friends, and Time:** As we have said before, your time will be limited when you work hard to set yourself up for future success. However, what matters most in life is not how much time we have but how we choose to use it. So, instead of focusing on many different goals, focus on just a few that will be the best use of your life. You may not have time for many friends. So, pick a few amazing ones. When with them, don't just pass the time. Use every minute to build deep, meaningful relationships. Schedule fun time with friends as much as possible. No matter how busy you get, go on an occasional outing. If you have a period where you have more free time than expected, be spontaneous and do something fun. Just remember your time with friends is very special. When with them, stay off your phone and remove your headphones. Listen, enjoy the moment, and bond.

The Power of Positive Values and Principles

Values and principles are your compass in life. Values are the *why* behind your actions, and principles are the *how*. For example, if you value hard work, the principle is always to give your best effort and avoid shortcuts. Without values and principles, you would be like a ship sailing without a rudder and compass. You would end up lost and out of control. When tough times hit, those without solid values crumble. But when your life is rooted in strong values, you can stand firm no matter what. Living by upstanding values gives you a sense of pride. It enables you to face life's storms confidently, knowing you're on the right course. A life anchored in strong values and principles is the ultimate goal, so below are a few for you to build into your life.

Getting Gritty

A fascinating study was done at West Point Academy, one of the most challenging military colleges in the United States. The study found that the biggest factor in student success wasn't IQ or physical strength. It was grit.[18] Grit means having the unstoppable courage to move toward your goal, even when it's tough, scary, and there is no guarantee of success. It is about staying in the fight, round after round until you win by being the last one standing, just like Rocky Balboa. Undertake a challenge that pushes your limits and helps you grow into a better version of yourself.

Long-Term over Short-Term

Every day, rewire your brain to focus on your long-term goals instead of short-term pleasure. Hit the gym instead of sleeping in. Eat healthy food instead of junk. Stay focused on your goals instead of distractions. Life is about pursuing what truly excites you. Find what pulls you toward greatness. As Tony Robbins says, "Pushing wears you out, but being pulled keeps you going." Our drive is building our family's legacies and combating worldwide financial illiteracy and the massive problems it causes. What drives you? Once you find it, go all in and let it pull you toward success.

Respecting the Gift of Education

Many students don't take school seriously and do the bare minimum. You have the opportunity to make the most out of the incredible gift of education by learning as much as you can inside the classroom and beyond. Even today, people fight and die for the right to an education. You have an obligation to honor their sacrifice and squeeze every drop of knowledge you can from your college experience.

Notes:

_____

_____

_____

_____

_____

_____

---

[18] MD, W. E. A. J. (n.d.). "Grit and uncertainty: Grit predicts performance and West Point graduation during pandemic conditions." *Military Psychology: The Official Journal of the Division of Military Psychology*, American Psychological Association.

Chapter 14 Workbook

1. Creating a Structured Routine

Create a daily and weekly routine. It should include your class schedule, study time, and personal activities like working out. What are the key elements of a successful routine for you?

_____

_____

_____

_____

2. Using a Planner Effectively

How will you use a planner (digital and/or paper) to stay organized with assignments and deadlines?

_____

_____

_____

_____

3. Avoiding Procrastination

What can you do to avoid procrastination? How can you get ahead of your deadlines to reduce stress and boost success?

_____

_____

_____

_____

4. Developing Grit

What will you do in the next 30 days to build your grit?

_____

_____

_____

_____

_____

_____

5. Staying Focused on Long-Term Goals

What is one long-term goal that pulls you toward success, even when things get tough? How do you stay focused on this goal amid distractions?

_____

_____

_____

_____

_____

_____

_____

_____

6. Values and Principles as Your Compass

What are the top three values that guide your decisions in life? How will holding firm to these values help you navigate challenges in college?

_____

_____

_____

_____

_____

_____

_____

_____

7. Living by Your Values

When have you faced a situation where sticking to your values was difficult but necessary? How did holding on to your principles help you make the right decision?

_____

_____

_____

_____

_____

_____

_____

Chapter 15: Accommodations

Understanding Academic Accommodations

If this chapter does not apply to you, feel free to skip it; however, if you are curious about accommodations, read on. Marshall had academic accommodations from middle school onward, which helped him tremendously. This chapter will help you see if you need accommodations. If you already have accommodations, this chapter will show you how to communicate your needs and make the most of your accommodations. Academic accommodations are adjustments or modifications provided to students with disabilities or learning differences to help them improve their quality of learning. They help students show their true abilities and have the best chances for success. Some common examples include extended time on exams, assistive technology, and note-taking services. By effectively advocating for your needs and utilizing available resources, you can enhance your learning experience and academic performance.

No Shame in Accepting Academic Accommodations

Accepting academic accommodations can be challenging for some, but there's no shame in it. A 2022 CDC survey found that 11.3% of US children aged five to seventeen (seven million in total) have been diagnosed with ADHD at some point.[19] Accommodations give you a better chance of success despite your challenges. Many students, even those hesitant to use them at first, realize how helpful they can be. For example, we had a peer in high school who faced academic difficulties. Despite his initial opposition, his parents encouraged him to get professionally diagnosed. He initially rejected the diagnosis. But, he later accepted it and embraced the accommodations, like extended time on assignments and exams. These accommodations allowed him to improve his SAT scores and have more success in his classes. They also helped him succeed in college, earn his master's, and gain professional certifications. His story is just one example of how academic accommodations can support a student's educational journey and lead to long-term success. It's common to feel embarrassed about needing accommodations, but they're not a sign of weakness. These tools help unlock your full potential, whether you're in high school, college, or pursuing professional certifications. It takes courage to ask for help, but doing so sets you up for long-term success, so don't hesitate to seek the support you need.

---

[19] Reuben, C., & Elgaddal, N. (2024, March 20). *"Attention-Deficit/Hyperactivity Disorder in Children Ages 5–17 Years: United States, 2020–2022."* Centers for Disease Control and Prevention.

Do You Need Accommodations? If you think you might need accommodations, look for these signs. If they sound familiar, consider getting a professional evaluation. A diagnosis isn't a label—it's a way to understand your needs and find the right tools for your success.

You Might Need Accommodations If You Have

- Difficulty keeping up with reading or writing
- Trouble focusing
- Processing delays
- Memory or retention issues
- Physical or sensory limitations

- Mental health challenges
- Learning disabilities or ADHD
- Fatigue or chronic illness
- Difficulty managing workload
- Anxiety in timed settings
- Frequent health-related absences

Types of Disabilities and Accommodations

1. **Learning Disabilities (Dyslexia, Dyscalculia, Dysgraphia):** Extra time, recorded lectures, and tech tools like screen readers.
2. **Mobility Impairments:** Accessible classrooms, adaptive seating, and note-takers.
3. **ADHD/ADD:** Extended time, quiet testing spaces, breaks during long exams.
4. **Autism Spectrum Disorders:** Extra time, visual aids, and quiet spaces for testing.
5. **Health Impairments:** Flexible attendance, extended deadlines, note-takers.
6. **Emotional/Psychological Impairments:** Reduced course load, extended deadlines, access to counseling.
7. **Hearing/Vision Impairments:** Sign language interpreters, screen-reading software, and large-print materials.

Types of Accommodations Elaborated

Learning Disabilities

Accommodations help students with learning disabilities perform better academically. Common accommodations include:

- **Extra Time:** Allows more time to process information and articulate responses.
- **Quiet Testing Environment:** Helps students concentrate by minimizing distractions.
- **Note-Taking Assistance:** Services like peer note-takers or note-taking software for students who need help capturing important information.

Physical Disabilities

Students may need accommodations tailored to their physical needs, such as:

- **Accessible Classrooms:** Ensures that all learning environments are accessible.
- **Assistive Technology:** Tools like screen readers or speech-to-text software.
- **Modified Equipment:** Adaptive classroom equipment that meets physical needs.

Mental Health Concerns

For students with mental health issues, accommodations may include:

- **Flexible Deadlines:** Adjustments to deadlines when mental health affects academic performance.
- **Breaks During Exams:** Allows periodic breaks to manage stress or anxiety during long exams.
- **Priority Registration:** Helps students plan schedules that meet their needs.

Preparing in Advance

Early Planning: Begin planning for accommodations as soon as possible. You may want them for high school, standardized testing, or the college you will attend. Contact your school's disability services office to start the process early. This will reduce the stress and complications of setting things up at the last minute.

Documentation: Be prepared to provide documentation of your disability or learning difference. This may include medical records, psychological evaluations, or a past Individualized Education Plan (IEP). Make sure your documentation is current.

Tell Your Teachers About Your Accommodations Right Away

Once your accommodations are approved, it's your responsibility to inform your teachers. Here's how to approach it:

- **Email Introduction:** Write a brief email to your teacher. Attach your accommodation letter and clearly outline your needs.
- **In-Person Follow-up:** After the first class, talk to your teacher. This will reinforce your email and help you connect.

Developing Self-Advocacy Skills

Self-advocacy is a critical skill. It will serve you in academics and throughout your life. Here are some ways to advocate for yourself:

- **Be Clear and Polite:** Communicate your needs directly and respectfully.

- **Follow Up:** If your accommodations are not being met, remind your teacher. If that does not work, immediately contact the disability services office. Let them know that your teacher is not honoring your accommodations.

- **Express Gratitude:** Acknowledge the hard work of your teachers and school staff. They have to work extra hard to provide you with accommodations. Showing appreciation fosters a positive relationship and makes people want to keep supporting you, which is a big asset.

Advantages and Disadvantages of a Quiet Testing Space

If you prefer to take exams with your classmates, discuss that with your teacher. Many teachers will give you more time. Others cannot because they have to teach another class right after the test, or another class is scheduled to use the room. Due to the cons of taking tests independently, Marshall always took tests in class when possible.

Advantages	Disadvantages
Fewer Distractions: This helps you maintain focus, especially if you are easily distracted.	**Lack of Immediate Assistance:** You may not have access to your teacher if the quiet testing space is in a different part of campus.
Reduced Anxiety: A calmer setting can help lower test-related stress.	**Feeling Isolated:** Some students feel disconnected from their peers when testing in a separate space.

Additional Tips for Success

Stay Organized: Keep copies of your accommodation letters, documentation, and any correspondence with the disability services office and teachers.

Seek Support: Reach out to disability services if you need additional guidance throughout the year.

Know Your Rights: Familiarize yourself with your rights under the Americans with Disabilities Act (ADA) and the Individuals with Disabilities Education Act (IDEA).

Use Your Resources: You will have the best chance of academic success when you understand your needs, advocate for yourself, get support, and utilize your resources. Accommodations are meant to help you reach your full potential. So, use them to your advantage without hesitation or shame.

Chapter 15 Workbook

If the following section does not apply to you, feel free to skip it.

1. Recognizing the Need for Accommodations

If you believe you might need accommodations, who in your school can you talk with to learn more?

_____

_____

_____

_____

2. Types of Accommodations

If applicable, what academic accommodations would help you most, and why?

_____

_____

_____

_____

3. Embracing Accommodations for Success

Can you recall a time when asking for help gave you the tools to improve your grades? How can embracing accommodations similarly enhance your college experience?

_____

_____

_____

_____

_____

4. Preparing in Advance for Accommodations

Why is it important to plan for academic accommodations before the start of the school year? What can you do to start planning today?

_____

_____

_____

_____

5. Self-Advocacy

How will you self-advocate when discussing accommodations with teachers or the school?

_____

_____

_____

_____

6. Communicating with Teachers

What will you do to let your teachers know about your academic accommodations?

_____

_____

_____

_____

7. Quiet Testing Space

What are the advantages and disadvantages of taking exams in quiet testing spaces? Would this type of accommodation help you, or do you prefer taking tests in the classroom? Why?

_____

_____

_____

8. Developing Organizational Skills

Why is it important to keep copies of your accommodation letters, documentation, and any correspondence with teachers or disability services? What can you do to stay organized?

_____

_____

_____

9. Using Resources Without Hesitation

What resources or support systems could help you reach your full potential in school?

_____

_____

_____

_____

Chapter 16: Achieving Success After College

Should You Get a Master's Degree?

Many college graduates consider continuing their education by pursuing a master's degree. Ideally, you should plan out your career before pursuing a bachelor's degree. A big part of that plan should be whether you need a master's or other advanced degree(s) after earning your bachelor's degree. In some fields, advanced degrees are required. In others, they are optional or unnecessary. To see if a master's or advanced degree is a good investment, weigh your career goals. Then, consider how much more money you would make from having the degree compared to the cost of getting it. Our website's financial calculators can help you decide if a master's degree is worth it.

Considerations for Pursuing a Master's Degree

1. **Program Costs vs. Career Payoff:** Understand the cost of the degree and whether the job opportunities and salary increase after graduation are worth it. Elite programs may offer better job prospects but will come with higher tuition fees.

2. **Choose a Program Aligned with Your Career:** Not all master's degrees offer the same value. Focus on reputable programs relevant to your field and career goals. Pursuing a degree just for the sake of having a degree is unwise.

3. **Balancing Work and School:** If you plan to work while pursuing your degree, seek flexible part-time or online programs. Some degrees may require full-time attention, making it challenging to balance them with a career.

4. **Employer-Sponsored Education:** Many companies offer tuition reimbursement or financial assistance for employees seeking further education. If you're employed, check if your company offers this benefit. It can significantly reduce school costs.

Before You Graduate: Essential Steps

Hit the Ground Running: Many graduates find themselves without clear direction after college. However, following these steps can help you land a great job and start your career with momentum.

Consider Internships: Internships provide valuable real-world experience, often leading to job offers. Start seeking internships early. They will help you gain hands-on experience and build connections. This will make it much easier for you to find a great job after graduation.

Letters of Recommendation: Strong letters of recommendation are critical when applying to master's programs and jobs. Build relationships with professors, mentors, and employers in college. By graduation, you should have done such great work that these people would gladly vouch for your skills, work ethic, and character. Request letters far before they are needed and provide your recommenders with useful information to help them highlight your strengths.

Resume Building: Start building your resume early. Gain relevant work experience and engage in events related to your career field. Update your resume as needed. Before sending it off, customize it for the job or grad program you're applying to.

Start Higher, Ascend Faster: Starting at a higher position gives you better opportunities to rise within an organization. Seek roles where senior management will see your work. This will lead to faster recognition and promotions. When negotiating your job title, duties, and salary, present a plan that clearly shows how you will meaningfully contribute to the company's success.

1. **Build a Strong Reputation:** Establish yourself as a hardworking, dependable individual. Peers, mentors, and professors who see your dedication will be more inclined to help you.

2. **Share Your Goals:** Be vocal about your career aspirations. The more people who know what you're striving for, the more likely they are to offer help and connections.

3. **Leverage Your Network:** Reach out to family, professors, peers, and alumni to expand your network. Networking is a powerful tool. Build more relationships, and you will find more opportunities.

4. **Find and Cultivate Mentorship:** Seek mentors in your desired field. Ask for guidance and actively maintain those relationships. Mentors can be a source of invaluable advice and connections.

5. **Pursue All Relevant Opportunities:** Keep exploring internships, volunteer work, part-time jobs, and interviews related to your field. Every bit of experience helps you refine your skills and improve your resume.

6. **Prepare to Impress Employers:** Thoroughly research potential employers, their industry, and competitors. In interviews, present ideas demonstrating how you can add value to their organization.

7. **Know Your Worth:** Research what your role typically pays using platforms like Glassdoor before negotiating salaries. Be prepared to negotiate a salary that reflects your experience and the market rate.

8. **Compare Offers Wisely:** When choosing a job offer, consider the value of salary and benefits. These may include health insurance, retirement plans, and professional development opportunities. Also, consider the company's growth potential, culture, local cost of living, and quality of life.

Getting Promoted and Asking for a Raise

Step 1: Create Value Before You Ask for It: Consistently demonstrate your value by going beyond the requirements of your job description. Measure your impact. It could be higher revenue, lower costs, or better processes. You need this data to justify your request for a raise or promotion.

Step 2: Showcase Your Value to Your Boss: Present your achievements and future plans to your boss. Collaborate on goals that align with the company's growth and set the stage for a raise and/or promotion.

Step 3: Ask for the Raise or Promotion: Position your request as a fair exchange for the value you bring to the company. Be specific about the raise you seek and account for inflation when negotiating. Inflation is how much the prices of things increase over time when more money is in circulation. So if inflation is 3% and you get a 2% raise, you will be paid more money, but you'll be able to buy 1% less. To improve your financial situation, ensure your pay is increasing more than inflation.

Step 4: Negotiate Effectively: Listen to your boss's feedback and be prepared to compromise or respond as needed. Be patient, and give your boss space to consider your request if necessary.

Step 5: Deliver on Your Promises: Once you've received the raise or promotion, continue to exceed expectations. Maintain open communication with your boss. Now, contribute even more to set yourself up for further success. Contributing more after a promotion will also make your boss feel they have made the right decision.

When to Change Jobs

Changing jobs too often can hurt long-term career growth. But sometimes, it's necessary to move on. Limited advancement, unethical behavior at the company you work for, or a better offer are all good reasons to switch. Always have a new job lined up before quitting. Leave on good terms with adequate notice to maintain your reputation. Don't burn bridges!

Foundations of Financial Literacy

Today, many people are taught how to earn money but not how to use it to set themselves up for success. They're stuck in a cycle of working hard, earning, spending, and starting all over again with nothing to show for it. Financial literacy breaks that cycle. It's the key to controlling your finances. It opens doors to independence and stability. Financial literacy isn't just for the wealthy. It's for everyone, and those just starting their careers need it most. If you're just starting to earn money, building a foundation of financial knowledge now will make your future far more successful.

What Is Financial Literacy? For many, the concept of financial success is wrapped up in getting a good job and earning a solid paycheck. But financial literacy goes beyond that—it's about understanding how money works and how to use it to make more. It's about knowing where every dollar goes and making sure that money is helping you achieve your goals. Being financially literate means:

1. **Knowing how to budget, save, and spend wisely.**

2. **Knowing the difference between assets and liabilities. Assets increase your wealth. Liabilities drain it.**

3. **Making informed choices that help your money grow and work.**

Why Financial Literacy Matters: To illustrate the value of financial literacy, let's follow the path of a man named Kevin. For Kevin, making lots of money has never been the problem. But his spending is a different story. Regardless of how much Kevin makes, he spends more. Kevin loves to travel, buy luxurious cars, crazy boats, big houses, and party. This out-of-control spending caught up with Kevin and caused him to build huge debts. Today, his debts are so big that he works around the clock just to stay above water. His stress is through the roof. We have no idea how he keeps things going or when it will all fall apart. There are countless stories of people who made tens of millions as actors or athletes. These stories often end up with the celebrity losing everything and going bankrupt. From these stories, it's clear that you can make tons of money but still be financially trapped. Why? Because money doesn't lead to financial security; it's what you do with it that counts. Without financial literacy, it's easy to feel stressed and overwhelmed by money, no matter how much you earn. The last thing we want you to do is work incredibly hard, make a ton of money, and end up broke. If you don't want that to happen, pay close attention to the following section.

Why You Should Love Financial Literacy: To gain control over your financial life, you need to understand the basics. Money flows in and out. How you use that money can either set you up for success or keep you running in place like a crazy hamster at a pet store. Here, we'll break down why you should love learning about financial literacy, then help you better understand the money you make and how to use it to set yourself up for a great life.

1. **Empowerment:** Money is a powerful tool, but without knowing how to use it, it can control you. Financial literacy gives you the power to make choices for yourself. When you control your finances, you gain a sense of independence and freedom, knowing you can navigate life's financial challenges.

2. **Avoid Becoming Enslaved to Debt:** One of the biggest risks, especially when young, is falling into debt—credit cards, student loans, car loans, and more. Poor financial decisions can trap you in a cycle where all the money you make is used to pay your debts. Financial literacy teaches you to avoid getting into bad debts that will suck your money dry. By freeing

yourself from debt, you can focus on building wealth and enjoying life instead of stressing day and night like Kevin in the previous story.

3. **Building Wealth and Security:** Financial literacy helps you grow your money and earn more. It aims to improve your quality of life and financial security. Start early. Invest time in learning how to manage your finances and grow your money. Then, you can work toward building financial security and, ultimately, financial freedom.

4. **Achieving Life Goals:** Financial literacy is your road map. It helps you save for education, travel, buying a home, and preparing for retirement. Knowing how to budget, save, and invest gives you the tools to reach your dreams, no matter what they are. It's the difference between wishing and planning, between hoping and achieving.

Earning Money

Your income is the fuel for everything you want to achieve financially. It dictates how much you can save, invest, or spend, which is why we are covering it first. You need to know the different ways of making money and how much you will have left to use after taxes and expenses.

Gross Income: This is the total money you earn before any is taken out for taxes and other deductions. Think of it as the starting point.

Net Income: This is what you take home after taxes, deductions, and work-related expenses. Your net income is the real money you can work with to save and spend.

How Much of Each Dollar Do You Get to Keep? Here's an oversimplified example of what usually happens with every $1 you earn. Most people get to keep about 50–70 cents of every dollar they earn after taxes. The exact amount depends on where you live, how much you earn, and what you buy.

1. **Federal Tax:** The government takes about 10–37 cents, depending on how much you make.

2. **Payroll Tax:** You lose 7.65 cents for Social Security and Medicare. Your employer must also pay another 7.65 cents to the government for your salary. So, the total cost is 15.3 cents. Your employer's part could otherwise go to you.

3. **State Tax:** Your state might take 0–13 cents.

4. **Sales Tax:** When shopping, you will pay 0–10 cents per dollar in sales tax.

5. **Other Taxes:** Let's not forget about property taxes, tolls, use taxes, licenses, etc.

Taxes are a fact of life. Knowing the basics about taxes helps you make better financial decisions. It can help you avoid surprises and take advantage of tax benefits. That way, you can keep more of your hard-earned money. You probably never learned about taxes in school. So, we have a free course on our website that teaches you the basics of taxes, including how to do your own. Available August 1, 2025.

Wages vs. Salary: A wage is paid hourly, meaning your earnings vary based on your work hours. A salary is a fixed amount you receive annually, regardless of hours. Knowing the difference can help you decide what kind of work best aligns with your lifestyle and financial goals.

Hourly Wages

Pros:

- You are paid for every hour you work and can earn extra money if you work more hours (overtime).
- Great if you like flexibility and want to work part-time or pick up extra shifts.

Cons:

- If you don't get many hours, your paycheck will be smaller.
- No pay for sick days, holidays, or time off unless your job specifically offers it.
- Your schedule might not be steady, so it can be hard to predict your income.

Salary Pay

Pros:

- You get the same paycheck every time, so planning your budget is easier.
- You usually get paid for holidays, sick days, or vacations, even if you don't work.
- Some salaried jobs come with benefits like health insurance or retirement plans.

Cons:

- You might have to work extra hours without getting paid more (no overtime pay).
- If the job is very demanding, you could end up working more than you expected.
- Your pay may not change even if you want to work more hours.

Passive Income: This is income earned with less direct work. It includes dividends, rental income, and royalties. It's the kind of income that gives you freedom. It keeps coming in, even when you aren't working for it. Building passive income streams is one of the smartest moves you can make to work toward financial freedom.

Developing a Healthy Money Mindset

Managing money effectively isn't just about numbers—it's about mindset. A healthy relationship with money starts with how you think about it. The next part is your habits and priorities regarding spending, saving, and investing. Here are some key principles for creating a positive money mindset to improve your finances, reduce stress, and boost your confidence.

Prioritize Needs Over Wants: Needs are the essentials for survival. Wants are the extras that enhance your lifestyle. When you put needs first, you're less likely to overspend and more likely to build financial security. It's not about depriving yourself. It's about setting priorities and making smart choices with your money.

Avoid Comparison: Feeling pressured to "keep up" with others is normal. This is especially true when you see friends or family buying things you want. But remember, everyone's financial journey is unique. Comparing yourself to others can cause financial stress. It may also distract you from your goals and lead to wasteful spending. Focus on what you need and want for your life, and let that guide your financial choices.

Reflect on Purchases: Before making a purchase, ask yourself if it aligns with your financial goals. This practice can reduce impulse spending. It will also help you make purchases that genuinely add value to your life. A great tip is to wait a week or longer before buying something in your online shopping cart. You may find, upon reflection, that you no longer want the item. Or, you may find a better, less expensive option.

Identify Financial Triggers: Know what causes impulsive spending. Is it stress, boredom, or social pressure? By identifying these triggers, you can build healthier habits. You can also find better ways to manage your emotions.

Celebrate Financial Milestones: Reaching financial milestones, such as paying off a credit card, building an emergency fund, or achieving a savings target, is a significant accomplishment. Celebrate these achievements. Recognizing your progress reinforces positive financial behaviors and motivates you to keep moving forward. In the pages ahead, we will walk you through how to reach each of those milestones.

Avoiding Lifestyle Creep

Lifestyle creep is a sneaky but powerful force that can derail your financial progress. It happens when your expenses increase alongside your income. It prevents you from being able to save and invest effectively. People often feel compelled to "upgrade" their lifestyles as they earn more. They want nicer cars, bigger apartments, and more luxuries. But, this mindset can stall their long-term financial goals. Avoiding lifestyle creep requires a conscious approach to managing both your income and spending. Here are some strategies to keep lifestyle creep in check:

Live Below Your Means: No matter how much you earn, spending less than you make is key to financial success. Living below your means creates room in your budget. You can then save and invest for your future goals. This habit helps you avoid the "earn more, spend more" cycle that often traps people in a paycheck-to-paycheck lifestyle, regardless of how much money they make, like Kevin in the earlier example.

Set a Savings Rate: Whenever your income increases, commit to saving a specific percentage of that increase. This ensures that a part of every raise or bonus goes to your financial goals, not just spending. For example, if you get a raise and make $500 more a month, save half. So, you are now saving another $250 a month. This approach boosts your savings and controls your spending as you earn more.

Prioritize Goals over Impulse Purchases: It's easy to be tempted by short-term wants, but focusing on long-term goals—like saving for retirement, a home, or an emergency fund—helps you stay disciplined. Clear financial goals give purpose to your savings. They help you resist impulse buys that can lead to lifestyle creep.

Building Good Financial Habits

Good financial habits are the backbone of a stable and successful financial life. When positive financial habits become routine, you'll stress less and achieve your goals faster.

Budgeting a Core Skill: Income fuels your financial goals, and budgeting is the map that helps you reach them. Without a budget, it's easy to overspend and let money slip through your fingers. Budgeting puts you in control. It shows you where every dollar goes and helps you make the most of your money.

The 50/30/20 Rule: This popular budgeting rule is simple and effective: allocate 50% of your income to needs such as housing, food, and utilities, 30% to debt repayment/savings/investments, and 20% to wants. Following this rule can help you balance living well today and preparing for the future. Adjust the percentages if needed.

Tracking Expenses: A budget only works if you know where your money is actually going. Apps like Mint and YNAB can simplify budgeting. They track every transaction, categorize expenses, and show your spending patterns. You can use Excel and Google Sheets too. Tracking gives you a clear view of your spending habits. It reveals areas where you might be overspending and helps you make room for savings.

Review and Adjust Regularly: Financial plans aren't static; they should evolve as your life changes. Life is, after all, unpredictable, and your budget should be flexible enough to handle that. Be ready to adjust, whether it's a new job, an unexpected expense, or a change in your goals. A budget should evolve as your financial situation changes, but always prioritize your necessities and savings.

Monthly Review: Set aside a time each month to review your budget. This review allows you to adjust as necessary, ensuring you stay on track with your goals. It also shows you areas where you might be able to cut back or save more.

Annual Financial Check-Up: Review your broader financial picture once a year. This "financial check-up" allows you to assess your progress and set new goals. It also gives you the chance to adjust your budget and investment strategies if your income or circumstances have changed.

Saving Money: Building Your Safety Net

Now that we have shown you how to make more money by getting a raise and saving more money by using a budget, you are ready to start building your emergency fund. This will be your first line of defense when financial setbacks occur. Save six months worth of living expenses. It will prepare you for life's surprises, like a job loss, a medical emergency, or a car repair. Without savings, a minor emergency can ruin your finances and make you desperate. We want you to have a savings safety net that will prepare and protect you so you can reach your financial goals faster with less stress.

High-Yield Savings Accounts: Unlike checking accounts or typical savings accounts, high-yield savings accounts offer higher interest rates, allowing your money to grow. While they won't make you rich, savings accounts provide a safe, low-risk place to build your safety net. They're designed to hold funds you don't plan to spend immediately but want access to if needed. This ensures that your money is readily available in an emergency. Check out our website for a free course on how to use your savings to set yourself up for success. Available August 1, 2025.

Pay Yourself First: This means saving or investing money as soon as you get paid. Do this before paying bills or spending. Decide how much to save each month and treat it like a bill that must be paid in order to buy financial freedom.

Avoid Raiding Savings: Protect your savings from impulse spending. Only dip into your savings for genuine emergencies. This discipline preserves your savings for the times when you truly need them.

Restocking the Fund: If you dip into your emergency fund, prioritize rebuilding it. Even if you can only replenish it gradually, the goal is to restore your safety net so you're prepared for the next unexpected expense.

Automate Savings: This is one of the simplest yet most effective ways to save for the future. Arrange for a portion of your paycheck to go directly into a savings account with direct deposit. This way, you are saving automatically without lifting a finger.

Debt and Borrowing

Debt is a double-edged sword—it can be a tool to help you achieve your dreams or a trap that holds you back. Debt is borrowing money now and promising to repay the money you borrowed plus a bit more later. When well-managed, debt allows you to achieve big goals like getting a college education or buying a home. Managed poorly, debt will drain your finances and make life far harder. Managing debt is essential to staying in control of your financial future. This is especially true for college students with multiple types of debt. The strategies we outlined, like budgeting, will help you save money so you don't get into any more debt and can pay off the debts you have. Now, let's dive into the basics of debt and how to make it work for you, not against you.

The Best Debt Repayment Strategy: The debt avalanche strategy involves paying off debts with the highest interest rates first. This is the absolute best strategy for saving the most money and helping you pay off your debts the fastest.

Negotiate with Creditors: If you're having trouble making payments, reach out to your creditors. Many will work with you. They may offer payment plans or lower interest rates. This is especially true if you show a commitment to repaying the debt. Negotiating can help relieve immediate financial pressure and make your payments manageable.

Avoiding Predatory Lending: High-interest loans, such as payday loans, may seem like quick fixes. However, their high interest rates lead to more debt. If possible, explore other options, set up a payment plan with your creditors, or seek help from a credit counselor.

Good Debt vs. Bad Debt: Many people are told that debt is horrible and that they should never have it. While this advice is well-intentioned, it is not helpful or realistic for many students who are just starting out and have limited resources. Whether debt is good or bad depends on how you use it. Before you borrow or spend, always ask yourself: "Will this help me succeed in the future, or will it hold me back?"

Good debt is when you borrow money to invest in something that helps your future. You spend money now, but it gives you big benefits later. For example, let's look at "Good Debt Grant." He borrows $100,000 in student loans to pay for college. After he gets his degree, he earns $25,000 more per year than he would without it. In just five years, Grant used the extra money he earned to pay back the loan and interest. After that, he still has forty-plus years of work ahead of him and will earn an extra $1,000,000 because of his degree! ($25,000 a year for 40 years = $1,000,000).

Bad debt, on the other hand, can hurt your future. For example, "Bad Debt Bobby" also borrows $100,000 for school. But his degree doesn't help him earn more money or get a better job. Now, he's stuck with a huge loan and no way to pay it back. He spent years in school, and now he'll spend decades paying off the debt he gained nothing from.

Interest Rates: Interest is the cost of borrowing money. The higher the rate, the more the money you are borrowing, aka debt, will cost you.

- **Federal student loans**, as of 2025, have interest rates between 6.53% and 9.08%. This means that if you borrow $100 for one year, you will pay between $6.53 and $9.08 in interest.[20]

- **Credit card loans** usually have very high interest rates, ranging from 20% to nearly 30%. This means that if you borrowed $100 for a year, you would pay between $20 and $30 in interest. Credit cards are much more expensive than other loans. So, pay off your credit cards and other high-interest debt first.[21]

Investing: The Key to Growth

While saving is an essential starting point, investing is the key to massive personal and financial success. Many people think investing takes tons of money and is super complicated. In reality, you only need a small amount of money to get started, and it can be as simple or complicated as you want it to be. What you need to know is that investing is not a get-rich-quick scheme. Investing is a long, slow journey to success. Starting August 1, 2025, our website will offer a free video course showing you how to set up investment and retirement accounts. We will teach you everything you need to know to get started and explain how investing just a few dollars each day can make you a millionaire by the time you retire.

Investing in Yourself: Investing in yourself means spending time, effort, and sometimes money to make yourself better, smarter, and stronger. It's like planting seeds for your future. For example, learning new skills, exercising, and eating healthy helps you become the best version of yourself. Working on your education, health, and talents sets you up for success later in life. Just like a tree grows strong and tall when cared for, you can grow to great heights when you work to improve yourself. Think about what you're passionate about or what you dream of becoming. The time you spend practicing and learning is like money in the bank being saved for a bright future. The more you invest in yourself now, the more opportunities you'll have to achieve your goals later!

The Power of Time: Many people wait until they are old to invest. That is the worst thing you can do. Every day you wait is one less day for your money to grow. And if you start too late, your money won't be able to grow enough to meet your needs. We want you to start investing as soon as possible because it will make a big difference in your future. You owe it to your future self to start today by checking out our investment course.

---

[20] *"Interest Rates and Fees for Federal Student Loans."* Federal Student Aid. (n.d.).

[21] Schulz, M. (2024, November 7). *"Average Credit Card Interest Rate in America Today."* LendingTree.

Chapter 16 Workbook

1. Should You Get a Master's Degree?

Do you think getting a master's degree would be a good investment for you?

_____

_____

_____

2. Letters of Recommendation

Who could write you strong letters of recommendation to help you get a job or be accepted into a master's program? How will the job or master's program put you on the path to your long-term career goals?

_____

_____

_____

3. Resume Building

What strategies can you use to build a standout resume while still in college?

_____

_____

_____

4. Building Connections

What steps can you take to build a network during college that will help you gain access to great opportunities?

_____

_____

_____

5. Evaluating Job Offers Beyond Salary

What factors, other than salary, will you consider when evaluating a job offer? How do benefits, company culture, and cost of living affect your decision?

_____

_____

_____

6. Getting Promoted and Asking for a Raise

What strategies will you use to create value at your job and effectively ask for a raise or promotion?

_____

_____

7. When to Jump Ship

When would you leave your current job for a better opportunity? How would you make the transition to avoid burning bridges?

_____

_____

8. Healthy Money Mindset

What are some current challenges you have with money? What will you do differently moving forward to achieve better results?

_____

_____

9. Building Good Financial Habits

What positive financial habits are you going to start today? Which do you think will be the most helpful for you and why?

_____

_____

_____

10. Debt

What is your plan to pay off any harmful debts you might have today and avoid bad debt moving forward?

_____

_____

11. Investing

After watching the investment course on our site, what is your plan to get started?

_____

_____

Chapter 17: Continuing Your Journey

By reading this book and applying its strategies, you are setting yourself up for an incredibly successful life. We've put tremendous effort into creating this book to help you build a strong foundation for lifelong success—but this is just the beginning. Take full advantage of the resources we've designed to help you excel in both school and life. Simply open your computer or smartphone and visit Atlasclass.com to get started!

Visit Our Website

On our website, you'll find links to all our social media accounts and our most up-to-date learning resources. You can also subscribe to our newsletter and stay connected with us on social media. As a bonus, we're constantly developing new online courses for our website, which will begin rolling out in August 2025. These courses cover essential topics, including financial literacy and life skills. We're committed to expanding our library of free courses, prioritizing the subjects our readers request most via social media. Additionally, our website offers resources for teachers, as well as information about our personal coaching and consulting programs, guest speaking opportunities, and the full range of products and services we provide.

Email us today to learn how we can help you achieve your biggest goals!

Contact: Info@AtlasClass.com

ATLAS CLASS

How to Hack College
Cut Costs in Half & Build A Foundation For Lifelong Success

Atlas Class, LLC
Email: Info@AtlasClass.com
Phone Number: (831) 293-4441
Visit our websites: AtlasClass.com
Visit our social media at: AtlasClass

First Edition: 2025
ISBN: 978-1-967158-05-8
LCCN: 2025915860

www.ingramcontent.com/pod-product-compliance
Lightning Source LLC
Chambersburg PA
CBHW081818200326
41597CB00023B/4294